THE TEACHER'S JOURNEY

Brian Costello

The Teacher's Journey
by Brian Costello

Published by EduMatch®
PO Box 150324, Alexandria, VA 22315
www.edumatch.org

These books are available at special discounts when
purchased in quantity for use as premiums, promotions
fundraising, and educational use. For inquiries and
details, contact the publisher: sarah@edumatch.org.

ISBN-13: 978-1-7322487-0-0
ISBN-10: 1-7322487-0-2

Dedication

First, I need to acknowledge my wife Lindsay, my daughter Emily, and my son Lucas whose love and support have been my strongest motivation for everything in my life.

This book is dedicated to my first mentors: my Mom and Dad.

Also:

To the late Richard Mathis, Dawn Skomsky, Sherry Bosch, Dr. Donna Van Horn, Phyllis Lopez, Amy Sack, Dr. Spike Cook, and so many others from Lower Township, Weymouth Township, and Egg Harbor Township who have helped me in my journey.

To the amazing students I have had the pleasure of working with over my career. You inspire me, and I can never thank you enough for allowing me to learn with you.

To the families who have trusted me with their children throughout my journey. I can only hope that as they become adults, I will have proved helpful in their journeys.

To Art La Flamme, who was my original inspiration for all my research and learning about mentoring and development.

To the seven incredible educators who were brave enough and willing to share their own personal journeys in this book.

To the all the other people who have helped make me the person I am today...

Thank you.

Table of Contents

Chapter 1

The Teacher's Journey

A Strange New World

On a warm September day, I walked into the first day of school for my new job as a permanent substitute. However, since no teacher is absent on the first day, the district placed us in specific buildings daily until we were called to serve in other places. Walking in that day, I wasn't sure what to expect. I felt nervous and excited as I entered the building. The walls were lined with colorful handprints of students and teachers that had come before me. I signed in and asked, "How can I help?"

Little did I know that I would meet someone who would affect the rest of my career. I was directed to guide new students into the building and help them find their classrooms. In truth, I felt useless because I did not even know where most of their classrooms were located. These wonderful tiny people came wandering down the hallway, some with faces filled with joy, others with fear. I helped some of them find their way, calmed some fears, and returned many smiles.

The next thing I was asked to do was unpack boxes of books, label them, and deliver them to classrooms. This may sound like torture to some people, but seeing kids learning in classrooms lit a fire inside me. This is where I was meant to be. In each room, I saw the excitement of young kids as they began their new year and the interaction they had with their teachers. This was my call to action. I had been chosen by education to serve its needs. In reality, I may have been called many times before and refused; it was only now that I was finally ready to embrace the call. Education has been lighting my fire ever since that first unassuming day, and it will continue to be a part of who I am until all my fires have been extinguished.

Fast forward three years. I had spent weeks during the summer getting everything ready: the room, the first day's lessons, the folders, desks, and boards. I was going to be the greatest thing that ever happened to kindergarten! These kids were in luck! I had so many great ideas, so of course, they were lucky to have me. I greeted each student one by one and gave them simple instructions to start the day. They were all smiling. I was, too. Working with my incredible aide and these bright young faces, I knew we were going to do amazing things.

That was the most positive and optimistic I remember feeling in those first few months. That euphoria was short-lived. As the door closed on my first day, I can remember feeling a rush of excitement that was quickly replaced with a sense of utter terror. It was a feeling I would come to know a lot in my first year, and one that would repeat on occasion throughout my career. It was a feeling that other teachers would later share with me as well: I have absolutely no idea what I am doing.

That wasn't entirely true. In retrospect, I was incredibly well-prepared. At times the chasm between being well-prepared and actually teaching is like the Grand Canyon. Despite all I had learned over those first three years in education, I still needed (and continue to need) to learn so much more. Since that day, I have grown tremendously as both a person and educator. At times I was merely treading water, wandering aimlessly through the depths and difficulties of teaching just trying to survive. At other times, I was overflowing with creativity, successful learning experiences, and gliding effortlessly toward success. The hot and cold swings were tempered by an occasional balance of struggle and success.

During all the ups and downs throughout my career, the most important catalyst for my success has been people. Too often we believe the myth of self-made success. Along the journey of every teacher, there are scores of unsung mentors, guardians, allies, temptations, and more who have shaped our path. As we learn who those influencers are and how they impact our development, we can gain an understanding of how we grow great teachers in the profession. Whether by fortune or by design, I am able to draw upon the many experiences of my life to help me and in turn positively influence others. There are many cases of exceptional educators that have walked the path toward success, and there are also many cases where the journey has defeated them. As we continue to reflect upon our own experiences and those of others, we will work together through this book to minimize those cases of defeat. Creating setbacks rather than endings means knowing ourselves and each other.

In communicating with many educators, I have found that I am not alone in my observations of these experiences and have come to two very important conclusions:

1. The education profession does not do a good enough job of creating and supporting the next generation of educators.
2. As a profession, we need to evaluate and improve how we create master teachers, starting from their pre-service learning experiences and throughout their entire career.

In this book, we will use the framework of Joseph Campbell's *Hero's Journey* to understand the how we become teachers and what enables the journey from novice teaching to mastery (1993). Throughout this journey together, we will discover more about who we are as educators and how we grow ourselves and the profession. As I share my own personal stories and those of many other educators, we will learn how our differences and similarities allow us to promote growth and success for all educators. I hope you enjoy the journey.

The Hero's Journey

"When I look back on all the crap I learned in high school, it's a wonder I can think at all." (Simon, 1973). This Paul Simon song may ring true for many of us, but one of the most vivid memories it conjures for me is Mr. Mathis's Humanities class. It was the first time I really felt challenged, not by content, but by ideas and passion. From a deep dive into Wagner's *Der Ring des Nibelungen,* a four-day epic tale told in German opera, to the quirks and creations of R. Buckminster Fuller my classmates and I were challenged to think. One experience that stands out above the rest was reading and watching Joseph Campbell, or "Uncle Joe," as Mr. Mathis called him. As we learned about Campbell, the monomyth, and the *Hero's Journey,* my classmates and I observed and discussed how these themes were pervasive in both modern and ancient storytelling (Campbell, 1993).

I can think of no better parallel to tell the story of developing educators than through understanding the ways that each of us is on our own personal Hero's Journey. The journey of each "Teacher Hero" carries its own unique story, but the overarching themes hold true. Understanding those themes helps us understand how we can be successful. Framing our own Teacher Hero in the light of Campbell's *Hero's Journey* helps us understand that success tends to come with struggle, effort, and help. We will see how my story and the stories of other educators fit this allegory. Before we do, however, let's explore the Hero's Journey in more detail (see the TED Talk, What Makes a Hero[1]).

After studying thousands of mythological stories from around the world, Joseph Campbell identified the common traits running through most of the world's great traditions and stories. While these stories are often fairy tales and myths, the format often holds true in the real world. Campbell provides numerous examples of how these stories fit into a common narrative. While their stories are unique, the underlying themes are prevalent throughout history.

The teaching profession is no different. No two teacher's stories are the same. What makes a story relatable is the ability to tell it with our own unique identity. Despite the commonalities in the legends, myths, and stories we tell, each maintains differences that allow us to connect with them on a more personal level. Campbell explores how each culture builds their myths and stories, but at their essence, the stories all follow the same cycle. We each play a role within our story filled with unique characters, situations, and challenges. Even with the vast differences in detail that make our stories unique, many common themes and experiences emerge amongst educators in their career at different points in their careers.

A hero's journey starts in the ordinary world. Our unsuspecting hero is simply living an ordinary life, or in our case, a life before teaching. Through some

---

[1] https://www.ted.com/talks/matthew_winkler_what_makes_a_hero

means, our hero is called to action. The hero is presented with a quest: a call to save or do good in the world. This calling isn't always accepted. Refusals are quite common as famous archetypes in the modern canon Luke Skywalker, Bilbo Baggins, Moana, Katniss Everdeen, and the Lion King's Simba demonstrate. Each one attempted to refuse their destiny, only to have that destiny thrust upon them in different ways.

At some point, whether initially accepted or otherwise rediscovered, our hero almost always takes the call and begins their journey by leaving the known world and venturing into the unknown. This beginning the journey is referred to as Separation, where our hero steps away from their status quo. Despite anything this hero may have done in a previous life, they are now thrust into a world of new challenges, new learning, and new obstacles. The hero must quickly learn the new rules of this unknown world to survive the repeated tests of their worthiness.

During this portion of the journey, our hero often meets with some supernatural aide, typically a being who has already mastered the experiences of the new world. This aide's guidance is crucial to the hero's development. The hero also typically finds helpers and companions along the way who will help them endure and potentially conquer the challenges that await. The hero's companions and helpers allow for the hero to learn more and grow into a stronger individual, before facing additional tests and a supreme ordeal. This part of the hero's journey is known as Initiation.

Each test along the way serves to make the hero

strong during this Initiation period. At some point in the journey, the hero undergoes an unusually trying situation. After having either succeeded in some way or not, the hero begins the portion of their journey known as the Return. The hero comes back to the ordinary world, but they are changed. Our hero is greater than before, and thus the ordinary world is different for them.

There have been many tests and ordeals in my own career and in the careers of other educators I know, but we rarely share these parts of our own journeys. So many of our teacher stories center around the ending. We focus on the final success more than all the learning and work that has gone into finding success. As a hero returns from this "other world" that was encountered, they are changed. Often our hero returns with something to show, some spoils of their journey that signifies change. In education, we often share the amazing achievements and the great triumphs without sharing the struggle that took place to reach those moments. The struggle is the journey. Many of you have heard the saying, that "it is not the destination, but the journey." Being a teacher is no different.

While triumphs are important to celebrate, the purpose of this book is to celebrate the journey itself and to understand how we move beyond survival to create more triumphs throughout our careers. As our journey progresses, we will see how current practices do not necessarily do enough to help teacher heroes to identify our supernatural aides and helpers (mentors and coaches) along our journey. I order to provide multiple opportunities to connect with ideas throughout your career, we will live this journey through the eyes of many teachers. I will suggest a different model for each vital step of the journey, with tips to improve and understand success in the midst of the journey. Through sharing stories of my own struggles and those of others, the journey through this journey will highlight common themes that either cultivated or stunted growth, enabling us to examine the steps that are likely to lead from mere survival to true success.

The Teacher's Journey

Each one of us has our own remarkable story. Our journeys through learning experiences, school years, and particularly our careers are filled with dramatic highs and lows. We survive remarkable challenges and meet unforgettable characters throughout our careers - and sometimes within the course of a single day! For so much of the history of Education, teaching has been a very singular, lonely profession. We close our doors and engage ourselves deeply in the work of helping young people. The harm in this isolation is severe. I never realized how isolated I was until I found other people who shared my ideas and experiences.

For over three years I worked as the oddball. I wasn't like the other teachers. Parents knew it, kids knew it, and the other teachers would occasionally make remarks that made sure I was aware of it. I wouldn't say the staff disliked me, but I clearly stood alone on some issues, which made me, as a newer educator, keep quiet. Even as a new teacher I believed in allowing my students to explore and learn through doing. My classroom was a shared space where most things belonged to the class rather than myself. Students in my room often talked, moved around, and I went out of my way to support them and give them opportunities for success.

I won't say that other teachers didn't do those things, but I was more to the extreme on many of those ideas. It promoted the type of learning I was hoping to see. A place where kids were creative problem solvers and were stretched beyond what they thought possible. I was learning and growing through my experiences and reading different ideas about student-centered classrooms and curriculum, but I had yet to really figure out how to be my own teacher. I was still being a watered-down version of Dawn, my first mentor and the teacher with whom I worked as an aide for almost two years. Dawn was a remarkable teacher, one of the best I have ever seen. I had achieved my goal of being almost half as good as her, but what now?

I started my master's program. In the program, I was introduced to Twitter by my professor, Dr. Spike Cook. I can't imagine how my journey would have proceeded without that life-changing experience on social media. With the touch of a button, I had access to so many educators to validate my voice, challenge my ideas, share their brilliance and sometimes even their failures. This is where I realized I wasn't just a lone oddity in the classroom. I wasn't by myself, just further away from my people than I realized. Why is that important?

Our journeys as teachers are personal and may have great differences in the details. Someone might argue that those details are what makes us who we are as teachers and as people. I wouldn't disagree with that assertion, but while our journey's details may set us apart, the commonalities are what can unite us. All of us have had moments of struggle and hardship and hopefully persevered with the help of others. As different as we are, there are many shared experiences upon which we can draw. These shared experiences can enable us to become strong mentors, to learn from one another, and to improve the profession.

These commonalities will serve as the focus for the remainder of our journey together. We will walk our hero's journey through the separation, initiation, and return. Within this book you will be able to see yourself at any stage of the journey, allowing you to see yourself within. Through understanding who we are as professionals, breaking through more than a century of historical isolation, and learning how our shared experiences can help others, we can build a better future: one that makes education better for ourselves, our profession, and most importantly, the communities we serve.

The Next Step

Over the course of this journey, we will be

stopping to reflect on the steps we take. I will ask you to stop and reflect on where you are, where you are going, and how you can get there. This experience was meant for all educators, so each stopping point will include questions and action steps for educators at different points in their journey. Sometimes you will be asked to reflect, other times to consider a plan of action. Each stop along the journey should ultimately help you to be more intentional and aware of your life as an educator.

During this first moment to pause and reflect, we can all do so together. As we go forward, you will find more specific reflections and strategies according to where you are in your own personal *Teacher's Journey*. Before going forward, I am challenging you to let go of your preconceived notions of heroism. Heroes are not necessarily people with superpowers, nor are they extraordinary in ways that differ from everyone else. A hero is simply the centerpiece of the story: a person who faces a series of trials (spoiler, we all do) and either comes through changed, or doesn't come through at all.

Educators are a remarkable breed. But, we also tend to deflect praise and feel discomfort with being labeled as special. This will pop up repeatedly throughout this book, so from here forward I am challenging you to read with the following things in mind:

1. You are a hero. Not in the "saves drowning puppies from a river" sense (unless you do that) but in the sense that this is YOUR story and despite how much

you give to others you are still the center of your own story. Start accepting it: in YOUR story, YOU are the hero.

2. Every one of us experiences trials, challenges, successes, and failures. Each experience is part of **your** journey.

3. Now reflect on what you have seen and done so far in education. For some of you, that is very little. For others, it is nearly a lifetime. At this point in the journey, it doesn't yet matter. We can all pause and reflect. Why education? What do I want next in life? What are some challenges I have faced? How have they changed me?

Think about these things. They will replay themselves throughout this book. Learning to find your path, to be intentional about improving yourself, and to discover how you can help others will all come back to these "Next Step" questions. Use these thoughts to help frame your reading as you go forward in the book.

Separation: Life Before Being an Educator

Chapter 2

Archetypes: Who Becomes a Teacher Hero?

In the ordinary world before teaching, we all went to school. Some of us may have had jobs or even careers beforehand. While all these things are valuable in developing our character and setting us on the path to our journey, these past experiences rarely prepare us fully for the unknown world we are about to enter: education.

We enter the field of education from many paths and diverse backgrounds. Even so, many of us share common attributes in our pasts that lead to success as educators. Whether you are a teacher, administrator, or support professional, you likely came to education with the desire to help others, to improve the world, and to do engaging work. How did we get here? What is it in our nature that drives us to pursue this profession? How do our different paths influence our needs in becoming master educators?

Each of these questions is an important launching point for understanding our journey. Knowing who we are and what drives us enhances our understanding of what enables us to grow. If we ignore the crucial aspect of knowing ourselves in relation to our profession, we are doomed to continue the path of single-serving learning that is disconnected from our goals. These one and done training sessions often fail to empower growth for much of America's education community.

Our diverse origins before the call to education can teach us about who we are as teacher heroes. You likely fit into one of the three general groups of people who go into education: those fresh out of school, those with some other work experience, and those who come to teaching as a second career. Each archetype brings with it unique strengths and areas of opportunity to the profession. Understanding the group means understanding its parts. Each journey is different, but there are common archetypal themes in our different worlds before education.

Not everyone will fit neatly into each theme, but understanding how a teacher comes to education can help us understand what challenges they are likely to face. What is most important to remember, is that we can see that great educators can emerge through any of these paths. Our differences allow us to have a special perspective, but we must also be mindful of how we support others throughout their career.

Lifers

We all know an educator, probably many within the profession, who will tell us how they have always known they wanted to be a teacher. As a child, they played school and thought, "this is who I am." These archetypal heroes have never refused the call. They knew at some point in their lives, early enough to make education their only career, that this was the path for them. Their experiences are uniquely within the sphere of education. Lifers look through these lenses as they engage in the journey. This group, who started their working life in education heard the call at a young age. If you are part of this group or are working with people who are, expect specific needs and common traits along this journey, especially when starting out.

This archetype in the journey is not mine, but like you, I know many teachers who are walking this path. I was fortunate to learn from their experiences along the journey as these teacher heroes shared their amazing stories.

Lifers walk into a classroom for the first time. Their entire lives have been building toward this moment. Sylwia Denko, an elementary teacher in Robbinsville, NJ, shares, "I had been waiting for this as long as I can remember...I took a moment to breathe it all in." This is quite possibly the only career a lifer has ever truly considered. Any other job before this one was just filler. With teaching being the focus for so long, finally achieving that dream is part exhilarating and part relief.

Sylwia had always known teaching was for her. She watched teachers and grew into the idea of being a teacher by wanting to emulate them. During her years before really starting her teaching journey, she would take part in extracurriculars that were school-focused, built classes for her family members, and tried to become the teachers she held in such high regard. This seems to be true of many teachers that come to education. The teachers who had always known they wanted to teach or had always had some draw toward teaching make up a large population of teachers in the profession.

I had the pleasure of meeting Sylwia just before she got her first shot at teaching. In speaking with her, it became apparent that she was going to be an amazing educator. Having watched her journey over the past several years, it is remarkable to see how quickly she has tackled the difficulties many of us took years to face. In part, her connection to the world of education coupled with her dedication to giving back has helped her navigate the journey so fiercely. This is one of the reasons I wanted to talk to Sylwia about her journey. Once I heard Sylwia talk about her positive school experiences and the lifelong exposure to activities akin to teaching, it was clear why she was drawn to education. It is likely that, if you fit this mold, as Sylwia does, your life experiences were heavily connected to teaching others.

Like Sylwia, Kory Graham, an Innovations teacher in Byron, Minnesota, had also decided upon teaching as her career for most of her life. "I used to play school and be the teacher." While many of us played school and imagined ourselves as the teacher, lifers as Teacher-Heroes answered this call and accepted it from a young age. In fact, Kory never thought she wouldn't make it as a teacher. "I always knew I was going to be a teacher, so it never occurred to me that I would try to be anything else." Interestingly,

Archetypes: Who Becomes a Teacher Hero?

Kory had the same teacher during three years of her early education and another teacher for two years. She vividly remembers having great teachers and their inspiring lessons. During the span of Kory's early education, her teachers' positive impact was so great that it influenced her toward a teaching career. She continued to find great educators in high school and again in college. Even in her small college in rural Iowa, Kory recalls having varied experiences with different and great professors who got her excited about teaching.

Kory Graham is one of the most inspiring, humble teachers from whom I have had the pleasure to learn. Her classroom is warm, caring, innovative, and exciting. I have watched and at times been a part of her journey. Kory claims to be "just a teacher," that she doesn't want any recognition, but what she gives to all of us in education goes far beyond her "just a teacher" moniker.

Lifers are special people for truly knowing what they want to do in life before they hit the age of 18. Most of us change our minds many times. Kory and Sylwia both attribute their desire to teach to incredibly positive school experiences. These lifers shared in the fact that they honored and loved teachers. Their path and willingness to accept the call was in large part influenced by that love. Many teachers share this experience, and reaching them in a meaningful way to create positive change in schools is hard. If you had these types of experiences, you and your coworkers are far more likely to accept the way things have been in your teaching and learning. There are still many lifers, however, who did not attribute their love for education to positive experiences with school.

Sometimes a call comes from positive experiences in working with others rather than a fond love of being a student, as it did for Rae Hughart, a middle school teacher in Illinois. "I grew up on the North Side of Chicago and was a dance instructor all through high school. It gave me some experience working with young kids and teens, so when I was looking for colleges, I looked specifically for a university that had a middle-level program."

Rae struggled in school; it was one of her least favorite things in the world and never clicked for her. Through her struggles, she found a passion for any teacher that would stick by her. That passion pushed her to want to support kids as a teacher that would work to find ways to help kids find their "Aha" moment. She loved working with middle-level kids and wanted to make a better opportunity for them.

While Rae is still relatively early in her career, she has become another example of how some of us on the journey are often better set up to become excellent. She has developed her teaching using a model called Teach Further around creating mini-internship style Project Based Learning (PBL) units. Over the past year, Rae has become a great example of how we can give back to the education community. She continues to work with her students, as well as younger pre-service teachers and other districts to share her learning and experiences. She is an inspiration to teachers who have joined the profession looking to change education, after beginning her experience with struggles as a student.

Like many of our other lifers, Stephanie Filardo, a high school math teacher in the St. Louis area, knew early on that she wanted to be a teacher from a mix of experiences of both good and bad teaching, as well as through working with others. She candidly remembers the support of her second-grade teacher being the original catalyst. "When I was in second grade my dog died. My mom sent a note. I didn't want to go (to school), but my mom convinced me I needed to go. Mrs. Klem understood enough of my social-emotional needs and set me up in the reading nook with markers and paper and just let me draw." Even as a young child, Stephanie recognized the impact that a teacher had on the lives of others, and it was the first of several inspirations.

Stephanie has continued sharing her ideas, her vision, and her experiences with the larger community of educators. Not only does Stephanie actively share her learning with teachers in her school, but also with educators from around the world. She has taught so many the value of recognizing kids' needs and providing them with resources so they can be successful.

Positive experiences with kids can be incredibly affirming. In some respects, it is a part of the call for many of us. When we love working with kids, we realize that teaching is ultimately our path. For our Lifers, positive experiences build them into the earliest acceptors of the journey. No matter its origin, following the call at a young age can bring a teacher both tremendous advantages and disadvantages in their journey.

All of your learning (or a large portion of it) is framed by your experiences. So, lifers enter the classroom with the possibility of the frame having been narrowed by a lifetime of following their call. The ability to arm yourself with knowledge and experiences that relate to being a successful teacher are some of the incredible benefits. However, gaining diversity in experiences can make us better as well. Strong teacher education programs, like those discussed by Sylwia and Rae later in the book, are essential to our development as lifelong teachers. Because of the importance of teacher education, our journey will take us through effective teacher learning and ideas to improve as we continue.

Lifers make up a significant portion of the teaching population, and there are so many opportunities for them to struggle, burn out, and leave the profession. However, many who embrace their journey from the beginning do not. They have always walked the path. Whether you are one of these teachers or not, understanding the journey from their perspective is important to being successful teaching and collaboration. You work with lifers and even for lifers, not learning how they grow will create a divide between you and the people with whom you experience your journey. We will talk much more about this group as they begin the journey.

Take Two

Like so many heroes before them, this next group of educators begins their journey by refusing the call, missing the call, or ignoring it all together. In these stories, our heroes experience the world of jobs outside of education and temporary careers that led them to finally accept the call. What did those experiences provide them? What experiences in their previous worlds pushed them to eventually accept their destined path?

As the son of a teacher and a child psychologist, I vehemently fought the call to education for many years. By the time I had graduated from college, I had given up on the idea of being a philosophy professor and knew I didn't want to be a lawyer. Beyond that, I had few ideas. My first job opportunity was as a financial advisor. I breezed through the classes and certifications (schooling and testing were never challenging for me) and soon found myself working fourteen or more hours per day, six days a week.

During those days I started out really putting in the work. I made cold calls, set up lunches to shoot sales pitches, and worked to market myself as much as possible. This may be the root of my general discomfort with marketing myself as an educator. While I believed in the value of what I was doing, helping people make sound financial decisions for their future, I quickly grew discouraged by what I saw. Not only had I developed all the tact of a smooth-talking car salesman, I realized that the people who were paying me for my advice were somehow worse than me. I was impressed by the people who could do this well, had developed good personal relationships with their clients, and were successful. I also knew that I had no desire to be one of them.

After less than a year, having recently purchased an engagement ring for my fiancée, I quit that job. I was liberated in a sense, but I also learned a lot about humility. I was a college graduate who had given up a career in business and could only find work as a waiter in a restaurant. Those were frustrating days. I have great respect for people who work in the food service industry as a career. I have worked in that industry for over twenty years, but always as a supplement, never as an end goal.

I learned a lot from working in restaurants. It teaches you how to talk to all kinds of people from all types of backgrounds. Having worked in both corporate and family-owned restaurants, I have seen a wide range of working conditions. By the time I started working in a school for the first time, I had worked for nearly twelve years in the service industry. I took a few lessons from that experience and continue to do so.

As a waiter, I learned to respect people who don't have the same educational background as me. I was born fortunate. While I didn't get to experience everything I wanted, I rarely needed anything and grew up with a host of opportunities thanks to my well-educated, dedicated parents. I was also gifted the ability to easily "play school." While I always had a curious, somewhat disruptive nature, I also knew how to play the game. Not everyone has that luxury. Working with, and many times for, people who did not have my academic background was, and continues to be, important. It has taught me to listen to, and communicate with, all different types of people. It has also taught me to respect the difficulties others face and allowed me to gain a greater understanding of people who are different from me.

Working in the service industry has helped me learn about efficiency. When working in food service, time and timing are how you make money. The more efficient you are, the more money you can make. In teaching, efficiency is equally important. In my first years, I learned to eliminate the things in my day that kept me from accomplishing what my kids needed. The lessons we bring to education from our outside experiences help shape who we become as teachers. Learning to leverage those lessons helped me become a better educator and survive my first few years of teaching.

While my story is unique, my path is one many have walked before me. Of the incredible educators with whom I have connected, there is a remarkable number who came to education in a circuitous fashion. Like me, they didn't hear their first call to adventures in education. They were either blinded by "bigger" dreams, or simply missed any signs that education would be one of their strongest professional suits.

Sarah Thomas, a Regional Technology Coordinator living in Northern Virginia, was not originally an educator. Though she wanted to be a teacher early in life, she lost sight of that vision. "It's funny because I wanted to be a teacher ever since I was a little kid. I wrote it in a book when I was in first grade, but it is funny because almost every job I had dealt with being with kids."

Despite wanting to be a teacher as a child, Sarah hadn't planned on going into teaching at all. "I was working for a TV station," she remembers, "and in fact, I worked for that station for a while." Then something struck her. "I was coming down the stairs from one of my master's classes and saw a poster for a program to become a teacher. I decided I wanted to check it out." From TV station employee and part-time recording artist, Sarah has moved through her education journey to become an incredible contributor to our profession. Through her work in schools, classrooms, and especially via EduMatch (her platform for connecting and sharing with other educators), Sarah has inspired many in our profession, myself included.

Similarly, Victor Small, Jr. had plans big plans to make his mark on the world outside of education. Victor (an administrator in Oakland, California), took a significantly different path than most to the classroom, yet having discovered where the values in his experiences lie, it has become a great advantage. What

28

did Victor do for most of college and early on before turning to education? He sold his music as a rap artist.

Unlike many teachers, Victor didn't jump into the classroom because of some long forgotten positive experiences with kids, but because he experienced what many of us experience after college: debt. With bills coming in, he needed a steady source of income that would allow him to continue to pursue his career in music. "I just sold CDs and performed when I got my first loan bill in the mail for student loans. That wasn't going to go away. A friend told me about substitute teachers that were making $175 a day. I didn't want to be a teacher until I first went there, and I realized I could do this, and it was a blast."

Victor took to the field of education almost as naturally as he took to music. Although he may have begun in the classroom for financial reasons, Victor has become an incredible force for good in education. His journey wasn't a straightforward path. He always believed he was going to go into a marketing field while he wrote books and poetry. During his time at school and shortly afterward Victor had become a recording artist. Despite marketing himself as a recording artist, he was hoping to use marking as a stepping stone to something else while he was performing.

Victor now works in Oakland, California where he champions Restorative Justice (a different way of looking at culture and discipline) and helps to build better paths for both his students and his teachers. As Victor's journey unfolded, I found so many similarities in our stories, in how we just showed up into the classroom and realized that not only could we do this as a career, but that we loved it as well.

Ultimately, like Victor, I found my love for education when I went back into a school and started experiencing the joy first-hand. Like our lifers, I found a feeling in working with kids that couldn't be replicated. It was a joy that I didn't find in other places. It took many years for me to find and follow that passion for becoming an educator, and along the way, I had many people who helped me. Through all of that, one of the most powerful memories I have in my developing teaching career was the feeling of struggle, of being afraid to share that struggle, and (despite knowing many educators) a feeling that I was in this alone. I have since found ways to break that isolation, but I can only wonder where my career may have gone if I hadn't needed to spend so much time learning how to get away from my deserted island mentality.

I am not alone in these experiences. Other educators have brought the experience of a previous occupation with them to the classroom. You may even be one of them. Many of us don't make the connections between their previous work and what they do now, but many do. Learning to understand how these past experiences make us better is a huge part of being successful on our journey. Powerful stories from educators who parallel much of my own story show how coming from outside of education can help us grow. Their ability to share their journey makes it possible for us to understand how many educators find teaching after making other attempts in the world.

There is great value to what educators with varied vocational experiences can bring to the profession. As we find our path and develop into becoming master educators, it is important to recognize and develop the strengths we bring to our profession. We ought to develop and share those ideas with others, to help new teachers see the connections between other fields and the teaching profession.

Our prior work experiences leave us with an incomplete understanding of the world we are about to enter. They do, however, bring us into the world of education, holding an interesting combination of experiences and biases which we must understand in a new context to be successful. While those of us that take this path can bring valuable ideas and experiences to education, we need a different type of help and guidance than a Lifer requires.

Educator 2.0

While our previous heroes found their call to education (see Chapter 3, *The Call to Edventure*) earlier in their lives, these teachers found their way to education long after their first career. 2.0 Educators worked entirely in another field, found some success there, but they were ultimately propelled into the journey. These heroes have seen the nature of one or more fields in the long-term. They bring a diverse and unique perspective of having worked in other capacities for a significant amount of time. As their stories unfold, our 2.0 Educators either finally acknowledge or experience a call to education. Their needs in transitioning to the classroom are different, and enabling them to thrive means understanding them well.

As I sought out teacher origin stories from the many educators I know, I was surprised to learn just how many of our fellow educators have come to education through another career. While we know some of these educators, it can be a shock to find out just how many of our peers have had significant work experience outside of the classroom. What finally brought them to work in schools? What were they hoping to get from their experiences? The answers to these questions help us understand our 2.0 archetype. 2.0 Educators are those that came from some significant career experience before finally answering the call to education. Our 2.0 educators share some common factors that have driven them to be successful in education.

Jon Corippo, Executive Director for CUE, Inc., was doing what he thought he wanted to be doing as he graduated college and moved into advertising. After thinking about teaching Physical Education in High School, only to have the original thought dismissed by his father due to monetary concerns, Jon went on to hold many positions in education. While he worked in advertising, he became more disillusioned that it wasn't the career he had learned in college. He didn't see the hands-on creation. Rather, it was something far less enjoyable. "I just didn't like how advertising felt as a business," Jon remarks. "You were always trying to get people to give you money, and then you couldn't guarantee them anything happened." This frustration with the reality of the field would pave the way for Jon to move into education and become an incredibly impactful member of the education community.

While some careers push us toward education because we become disillusioned, others push their teacher heroes toward the call because of their similar experiences and outside factors. Stacy Lovdahl, an Instructional Technology Facilitator and Teacher on Loan in North Carolina, got her start as a safety consultant. She consulted on the handling of hazardous waste within Cadillac plants for General Motors to ensure compliance with new environmental regulations. Stacy gained several useful experiences that slowly guided her towards a successful education career.

As Stacy's career progressed, she moved from Detroit to southern California to work as an environmental consultant. Stacy had been through the experience of trying to shift the outdated practices of those who defended the "we have been doing it this way for years" mentality. She also learned to work as an intermediary between regulators and clientele in environmental consulting. Stacy relates these experiences to her current work in education. "Being in that intermediate position between regulators, and having the pressure to serve my clients correctly is reflective of being a teacher where you serve your students and multiple stakeholders at once." While Stacy had so many of these experiences, she hadn't ever thought about how they crossed over into her teaching career until I asked her to reflect upon them.

Our 2.0 Educators bring many great work experiences to the table when they become educators. Some skills translate into the classroom extremely well. Other experiences may not cross over. Because of their tremendous life experiences, 2.0 Educators bring unique qualities to the classroom. With those unique qualities come differing needs in teacher development. If you came to the profession from a previous career, learning to identify what carries over, learning to build relationships with kids, and navigating the different landscape of a school are all important challenges. If this isn't you, you undoubtedly know some educators that held other careers before teaching, even if you don't realize it.

Why it Matters

Why does it matter where and when we answer the call? Our experiences lead us to find various entry points into the world of education, and they bring us there with differing needs. While we come from many different places, the many similarities in each archetype guide us to success in education. As educators, we come from many backgrounds. That variation provides us with different strengths, as well as blind spots. Understanding both provides us a path toward growth and success as a master teacher.

It is difficult to understand our needs and those of others without understanding what we already have in place. Most new teacher programs that exist are developed with a cookie cutter mentality. Emergency certification programs and postgraduate programs shorten the experience down to a minimalistic approach. In many ways, nearly all teacher professional development mirrors the mentality that provides everyone with the same learning. Districts tend to send all of the educators to the same trainings with no regard for what each teacher really needs. While I see this slowly changing, it is still the reality of too many educators who are trying to grow and improve along the journey. So, we start our journey understanding that there are several different archetypes for answering the Call to Edventure. Understanding the similarities and differences along the journey allows us to grow.

The Next Step

As I mentioned at the end of the first chapter, we are going to start seeing some more specific distinctions based on your personal experiences as we reflect and progress through the journey. In this section, I laid out the different paths to education. While you may not fit perfectly into one of these archetypes, the similarities are surely significant. Each archetype will have its own reflection to explore. While I encourage you to consider and explore all these questions to help you better understand others in their journeys, these reflections are for you. Not only now, but as you move through your own journey, they can be helpful stopping points to remember who you are, who you want to be, and how you can get there.

Consider the following reflections and challenges:

Lifers

1. Do you still remember why you got into teaching? Does your practice reflect your "why"? If not, how do they differ? If they are still similar, what have you done that helps you maintain that?
2. What experience do you have with non-teaching workplaces? What experiences can you take from those roles that can make you a better educator? If none, who do you know in education that has had significantly different experiences? Find them and see what you can learn about other fields and their skills and strengths.
3. What other identities do you have besides educator? In what way do those roles impact how you view teaching, your relationships with kids, and your ability

to give back to the profession?

Take Two

1. What did your previous career attempts teach you about yourself? Why were they unsuccessful? What parts of your previous careers can you transfer into your teaching, learning, and sharing with others? Each step in your journey has allowed you to reach this point. Take pride in and reflect on what you've done, even if you were unsuccessful in it, and use it to grow.
2. What about the teaching profession still doesn't make sense to you? What experiences did you miss by taking a less traditional route into education? Who can you learn from that will help you gain that perspective?
3. What made you turn to education? What characteristics of the profession have enabled you to stay? How is that reflected in what you do as an educator?

Educator 2.0

1. What prompted your career move to education? How does that reason for moving to education impact your daily practice? You should be able to keep your "why" in focus as you grow in your career

in education.

2. What have you learned from previous workplaces and careers? How can you use those experiences to benefit the kids and educators in your school community? You have had many experiences that can benefit others. Simply by understanding how the places you have been and the things you have done can apply to your work, you bring a unique and powerful perspective to any school.

3. It is likely that because of how you came into education, there are things you missed. These are things that won't prevent you from being a good teacher, but they are perspectives and bits of information that can make you better and also make your life easier. Who can you reach out to that comes to education from a different path that can help you understand these differences? What gaps might you have in your learning and how might you bridge those gaps?

Chapter 3

A Call to Edventure

Many people say that education is a calling, not merely a job. People claim that education is part of who they are as individuals. If that is true, how do we know? For me, it was simple. Working in a school was the first place I ever felt like what I was doing mattered. In a broader sense, any job can matter. The reality is, I needed something more concrete. The abstract sense of why my previous jobs were important didn't mean much.

When I delivered books to classrooms on that first day, while I was directing traffic for excited, frightened, or even crying young children, I knew I belonged. At the time I didn't really understand why it made so much sense, I just knew that I was in the right place. From that moment on, all my professional work was in pursuit of becoming an educator. Between then and now, I have had several other career options, including many opportunities to leave the education profession. For a variety of reasons, I have remained. Throughout every step, I can recall the people who have cultivated that calling.

Finding your call is often how we come to our profession in the first place. Having an inner passion that drove us to the field does not remove us from being professionals. You may have heard your call as a young student in some powerful moment with teachers, you may have moved toward education haphazardly and, like me, purposely avoided it. Regardless of the path you took on your journey you were undoubtedly called by something toward the profession. While my call to action on this journey took many years, other stories demonstrate both the diversity of our experiences and the common themes in our journeys.

The call is different for each of us. We find our path to education, our Call to Edventure, in many ways. While these stories may be varied, they hold some common themes which we can explore. Origin stories help build our identity. It is important to consider what made you want to be a teacher to identify the WHY of your teaching experience.

Sometimes, especially when times are at their worst, it is helpful to remember that origin story and reclaim your "why" for being an educator. Focusing on that "why" will give you an opportunity to remember the joy and excitement you felt in wanting to become an educator. A foundation of "why" set the stage for the growth and change our incredible teacher heroes have experienced in their careers. Knowing your "why" gives perspective not only on who you are, but the way in which you were able to move toward being a successful educator throughout your career.

It would be easy for me to look back at my career and think about how I made it to where I am through my own hard work alone. There is a part of that story that rings true. It would, however, be frightfully naive. It wasn't just a calling, it was a continuous drive toward improvement. My call wasn't just one moment, but calls repeated over time. I continue to grow into new areas because of new calls.

Along each step in my journey, there have been people empowering my growth. I may have experienced a moment of clarity on that first day working in education, but it was the repeated moments spared by those who invested in my development that changed me. Without each one, I would not be an educator today. I know my story is not unique. I can look back on no fewer than seven individuals who enabled me to simply begin my career.

I came to education from less than a year as a financial advisor. While I am sure a career as a financial advisor is an enjoyable, fantastic path for some, for me it was the worst job I had ever held. I have worked at ice cream shops, retail stores, and done nearly every job in various restaurants, but working as a financial advisor was the least fulfilling, most emotionally draining job for me. I left that job with little hope or understanding of what I would do next. It wasn't until I was feeling incredibly frustrated and disillusioned with the work world that my fiancée directed my thoughts toward teaching. She knew I liked working with kids and told me to give substituting a try.

As I shared earlier, my first day was the first time I really heard and accepted of my Call to Edventure. That call repeated itself many times in those first three years. During that time, I found my path. While directing traffic in the hallways and unpacking boxes were the beginning, I realized quickly that I was in the right place. Not only was I somewhat good at working with kids, I absolutely loved it. It became clear: being an educator was what I was meant to do.

I spent the majority of that first year in several long-term subbing positions, all of them in the primary grades. I finished the year with Dawn Skomsky. Dawn was an inclusion teacher that looped with her classes from 1st to 2nd grades. She was one of the best teachers I have ever known. She created engaging activities, fostered independence and growth for all her students, and built amazing personal relationships with her students and their families. **I wanted to be her.** If I could have picked a teacher to emulate, it was Dawn. I asked to be paired with her the next year, so I could stay with the class and learn from her. Dawn was my first real mentor, my first real coach, and one of the most influential people in my early practice.

From the experiences of others, I have seen a few common themes in how and why we become teachers. All our teacher heroes fit into one of three categories. Insight into their stories helps us understand their motivation for becoming a teacher and frames their growth and development through their careers. In each case, it is valuable to begin with their "why."

Our *Teacher Heroes* Hear the Call

One category of teachers is those who were positively impacted by the educators during their school experiences. These are teachers who can recall specific teachers and moments in school that led them to want to emulate the amazing educators that had an impact on their lives.

Kory Graham began to understand that teaching was her passion through the power of positive relationships her teachers made at a young age. She had the benefit of working with two of her PreK-6 teachers for five of the eight years she was in the school.

"I had pretty amazing teachers from kindergarten all the way up through college. I liked school, for the most part, all the time. I had teachers that really cared about their students and went beyond just teaching us what they were supposed to teach us." She also reflects positively on engaging learning experiences about a teacher who brought lessons to life by "having us sew Revolutionary War patches, and re-enactments" and learned through hands-on activities.

Kory, who is an incredibly caring and innovative teacher, developed a love of teaching through experiencing caring and innovating teachers in her early educational career. It is not surprising that Kory has always wanted to be an educator.

Sylwia Denko wanted to be a teacher for as long as she can remember. Her love for teaching was built on love and respect for the people who invested their time in youth. "It comes from watching the teachers and learning about different careers. It comes from thinking, I love this person so much, and I admire them, and I want to be exactly like them."

Sylwia's passion for helping young people grew from those experiences early in life. She has worked hard to become an educator that children will love, and everyone can admire.

For Stephanie Filardo, there are two versions, a "fluffy version" and a "gritty version." In second grade Stephanie's dog died. As it is for anyone, losing a pet was devastating for Stephanie, and she struggled to find the motivation to go to school the next day. Her teacher understood her social and emotional needs and let her sit in the reading nook. She gave her some paper and markers and just let her draw. It was the first time she really admired a teacher.

"It was the first time I realized the impact a teacher could have on someone's life." Early on in her career, she realized that being a person first can change the lives of the people with whom we work. Sometimes it is easy to get wrapped up in content, learning objectives, and other focuses of education. Our strength, and the strength Stephanie experienced from her second-grade teacher early in life, is that in teaching, relationships matter. Sometimes putting aside the lofty aims of educating kids and being compassionate, sympathetic, and understanding are what make all the difference.

Later, in her middle school math classes, Stephanie found both joy and talent for teaching by spending time as a student in class explaining concepts to other students. She enjoyed it so much so that she earned her first and only detention for talking in class. She earned detention for teaching others! This was the wakeup call that really let her know: teaching was for her. She realized she could do better to reach kids, treat kids as people first, and make a positive difference in their lives. Stephanie has embraced that approach over her career, and she has combined her dedication to students and her love of helping others understand math.

Stephanie's story fits both the positive and the negative side of being inspired toward education. She had experienced the best of what teachers could be, but also saw that there was room to improve. Some of our teachers were inspired by experiences in their educational career that made them want to improve teaching and learning for kids in a variety of ways. While admiring the positive is one important theme in teachers finding their path to education, seeing what is needed to improve and finding ways to make the experiences better for others has also proven a powerful motivator for many teachers.

Rae Hughart struggled with school early on. "It was about my least favorite thing in the world." She was classified as a special education student and had several difficult experiences in school. While Rae had some outstanding teachers, school was not something she loved. After she moved through middle school and into high school, she started to find the things that worked for her. Her experiences struggling in school inspired her to want to find "a teacher who could stick by me. So, when it came to what I wanted to do in the future, I really wanted to pinpoint those students that struggled like I did and give them the support that I feel I didn't have when I was in school."

Rae was inspired to help other kids learn to find it as well. Rae's current teaching reflects a desire to empower kids to use learning, to experience education in different ways, and explore real problems to apply what they know. Her style reflects a desire to help kids who struggle to learn traditionally.

Dr. Sarah Thomas knew she wanted to be a teacher by the time she reached first grade. Nearly all her experiences were centered around working with children, yet "somehow I lost sight of that along the way." Sarah built her love of working with kids through rich experiences. When she reached college, her mom started teaching middle school. "I would often go down to her class and help her set up. One day I was talking to the Library Media Specialist, and I told her one day I was going to have that job." She has spent a large portion of her career working with educational technology and media. Sarah's experiences teaching kids were positive, but her experiences as a student within the school system were not always the same. During much of Sarah's school experience, especially during high school was difficult. "I felt isolated, invisible, ignored, and like people didn't want me to be there. I feel like now social media has opened up a whole new ballpark. If you are feeling isolated, you can create a whole new network. They become friends, and they are so valuable to your life." The isolation of struggling to find her place as a minority woman in predominantly white advanced track classes, in a suburban high school outside Washington DC, combined with the same feelings of isolation early in her career have driven Dr. Thomas to build not only her own vast network of meaningful personal connections, but to help enable others to do so as well through EduMatch.

Like myself, many teachers entered the field because of an outside push. I was determined not to become an educator. My parents were both educators, and while I had tremendous respect for them, it wasn't something I ever aspired to do. In fact, I actively avoided the possibility. In college, I thought about being a professor. However, the initial arrogance I showed as a sophomore by taking upper-level philosophy classes without the prerequisites because "I'm smart" put a major dent in any chance of that happening. I continued to look toward business and had basically only ruled out doctor, lawyer, and teacher as my possible careers. Like many others who got a shove from the outside world, it was when I finally started working in the school that I found my love for education.

Jon Corippo's original desire to become a physical education teacher was brushed aside by his father's concerns that he wouldn't make enough money. After going into advertising because he loved the hands-on aspects of making and creating advertising plans, Jon soon realized, "that's not how the real world works, and

I just didn't like how advertising works as a business."
After falling in love with and marrying a teacher, he met
one of his wife's friends. This friend, a
superintendent, suggested that Jon become a teacher.
Several months later Jon acted upon that suggestion,
and that superintendent helped him get a job teaching
technology in his school district. Soon after, "I started
my first class as a long-term sub, and I was hooked
within three days." Jon fell in love with education and
making teaching and learning better by being in the
classroom.

Victor Small, Jr. was also given a shove into the
classroom. Not only were some of his friends working
as substitutes and making money, but he was also
pushed into working in the school by necessity. Bills
and loans were more than he could afford working only
as a recording artist and selling CDs. It was while Victor
was substitute teaching that he realized, "You know, I
could do this," and found himself with a long-term
substitute position because of a teacher shortage.
Victor found his love of teaching when he
entered the classroom; it wasn't something that came to
him from his childhood. Despite that, Victor's life
experiences have influenced him in his work with the
students who need him most. His everyday experiences
in difficult but rewarding situations using Restorative
Justice, combined with strong teaching practices and a
genuine personality have been staples of his career.

Stacy Lovdahl wasn't a teacher, nor did she think

she would become one. Becoming a teacher came from a dramatic shove into a field that allowed her to stay closer to home. Stacy had a family, an enjoyable job working as an environmental consultant, and was doing fairly well. She decided to reduce that lifestyle to stay home with and start raising her children. Changing careers didn't occur to her until her family was faced with a new hardship to overcome when her husband was diagnosed with Multiple Sclerosis (MS). This diagnosis brought about a shift in Stacy's situation: "It completely changed everything. I wasn't going to be able to be the stay at home mom we had downsized our life to create."

Stacy decided she needed a career that required more stable hours and more availability to help with her family. "It is going to sound naive because it was, but I was looking for a career that was family- and kid-friendly." Like many of us who get an unexpected boost into education, Stacy realized that she was really going to be an educator by getting into the classroom. Stacy's career has moved forward from that point with a strong sense of connection and dedication to other teachers, no doubt because she credits the help from her peers early in her career for enabling her to succeed.

Different and the Same

All of us have our own unique circumstances, but no matter how we accepted our "Call to Edventure," we came to find a love for school, for making ourselves better, and for making education better as a whole. The stories of these incredible master educators are important. They will show throughout the rest of this book how similarities can help us understand how to make connections to help grow ourselves and others.

All of us found our passion for education in the same place: the classroom. No matter where an educator may go in life, remembering the love for education we found in the classroom is important to continued success. Despite finding that love at different times and in different ways, there are many commonalities that we share, and that will help us forge a better path forward for others.

The Next Step

This chapter is truly about your "why." We have walked together thus far and focused a lot on who you are and how you came to be here. While the upcoming chapters focus on the buildup to your career in education, this one focuses on your "why." Why did you become a teacher? When we refer to our *Call to Edventure,* we are really talking about finding our purpose for being an educator.

Rather than breaking this apart by your archetype, much of the reflection going forward will break down based on where you are in your journey. Are you a pre-service teacher? Are you in your first year or two? Are you a junior teacher who discovered themselves as an educator but is still learning how to make all the moving pieces work in the most effective way possible? Or, are you a master teacher? Have you learned who you are as an educator, how you fit into your class, school, and educational community?

Consider the following reflections and potential actionable steps. As always, I urge you to think about the questions and ideas put forth for each group. Not only will they help you understand where others are in the journey, but they can also help you reflect on where you have been.

Pre-Service Teachers

1. Why do you want a career in education? What dreams do you have about being a teacher? How do they compare to the experiences you have had so far?
2. Once you have your "why" and you have thought about what you hope for as an educator, start planning how you might help keep your focus in the face of stress and struggles. What will remind you of the reasons you chose to be an educator?

New Teachers

1. How has your early experience in education differed from your expectations and your hopes and dreams entering the profession? What steps can you take to bridge that gap?
2. Now that you have some experience in the classroom, start to think about who

you want to be as an educator. Make a list of answers to the following:

    a. What do you value?

    b. Who do you want to be as an educator?

    c. Who are your role models? How often do you speak with them?

Junior Teachers

(You know who you are as an educator and you are well on your way to getting there.)

1. What do you need to continue growing? How does this vision fit with your reason for becoming an educator?
2. Take some time to write down what you do well. Make sure to include how you can maximize those skills in your teaching. Think about how you might be able to help others through what you do well.

Master Teachers

(You are able to use what you do well to improve your students, your colleagues, and your school. Let's reflect on your path and process.)

1. Do you still remember why you wanted to be a teacher? Is that still part of what motivates you today? If so, how does your "why" connect with the way you influence others in your school? In education as a

larger community?

2. Make a list with a focus on why you are a teacher. What do you do right now to improve education? How does that fit in with your reasons for being a teacher? Start to think about the influence you have in your school, and in the profession. Decide how you want to use your influence to make positive changes for others. Think about why that is important to you.

Chapter 4

How We Educate New Teachers

What Do Our Master Teachers Have in Common?

As I stated near the beginning of this journey, being *prepared* for teaching and being *ready* are two vastly different things. But why? Why are our newest teachers being dropped into the classroom and left to fend for themselves on the island? As a profession, education tends to struggle to hold on to its promising young talents. Some might point to low pay or increasing difficulty as reasons new teachers burn out or switch careers within the first four years (Bouffard, 2017). While those are certainly important factors in retaining talented people in the field, I don't know any teachers who enter the profession expecting exorbitant salaries or an easy ride. If they are allowed to believe this falsehood throughout teacher preparation programs, then we are doing them a severe disservice. How then do we create teachers who understand the challenges that await them? There isn't a simple answer, but many components that can come together to make great educators.

As the many origin stories of master educators have shown, great educators can bloom from anywhere. Taking from those origins, we can identify several important factors that help our educators grow from beginner to master teacher. Some key characteristics that all these educators possess seem to be universal whether they started out in the field or came to the profession later in life.

Our teacher heroes have cultivated these skills to succeed. As your own journey begins, you should also seek to:

Be curious. Great educators are always looking to learn. Looking to learn does not simply mean about their craft, but also about anything that interests them. We need to help prospective teachers foster this curiosity. It doesn't mean every teacher needs to be up on all the latest trends for everything. What it means is that our educators are demonstrating the desire to learn new things for their students, as well as in their lives. Part of every educator program should be the encouragement for pre-service educators to explore their curiosity. They should be encouraged to learn about fields outside their own and demonstrate their ability to explore diverse interests. Teachers who have multiple interests and demonstrate a willingness to explore and learn will be most likely to become master teachers, avoid burnout, and provide the best opportunities for kids.

Fostering curiosity in teacher education is a challenge. As with nearly everything else in the education field, the trend has been to increase the difficulty to increase the quality. While some improvements in the ways we educate new teachers are certainly necessary, we cannot foster better teacher development simply by making it harder to become a teacher. Instead, we need to make becoming a teacher a process that engages our next generations in an all-encompassing way. As we encourage new teachers to find their passions both in and outside of education, it is crucial that we teach them to be good, well-rounded, curious, and balanced human beings, not just good teachers.

Be humble. I don't mean to say you cannot advocate for yourself, think highly of your work, or tell your own story. By all means, all educators can promote their work and share it with the world. What being humble means is that we as educators are not the lead role in every story, but rather part of the supporting cast in each child's own hero's journey. Each one of the incredible master educators mentioned in this book is humble in this way.

They always view their work as "in progress." They view education as a good thing, but also something that will always need continual growth and improvement. Like their own craft, they see education as something that can always be better. Being able to understand that their craft is never perfected, and learning to support others in their pursuits, are elements of what makes a great yet humble teacher. Instilling this sense of humility in teacher education programs isn't something revolutionary, but we need to be intentional about how we teach these important concepts. Finding our way in education is challenging; focusing teachers on being in a state of constant growth so they can foster similar habits of mind in their own students is essential to the future of our profession.

Be reflective. Reflective practice has become a significant part of what educators to do be successful. In fact, it has been a part of great teaching for far longer than I have been involved in education. Thinking about what we do well and what we can improve are both essential to improving as a teacher. Getting new teachers to find time to be intentionally reflective requires making it as much a part of their practice as lesson planning. During student teaching, observations, and throughout any teacher preparation, the act of reflection through discussion, writing, and other means should be refined to improve teaching. With the myriad of tools available for educators to practice their reflection, the act of being reflective should be second-nature.

Be caring. Perhaps the most important thing an educator can be is caring. Yes, your content is important. Yes, the WHAT you teach is important. Caring for kids is at the heart of any master educator. Each of the master educators in this book cares deeply about kids and their ability to get a meaningful education.

Part of the *"Call to Edventure"* (in other words, the realization that you want to be an educator) should have its roots in a genuine caring about kids. While I know my own path included enjoying working with young people, I know from firsthand experience that the job can either build upon or tear apart your love of working with children. A person with a strong sense of caring for others, specifically for kids, will likely be the kind of teacher who grows into loving the profession, rather than one who will become jaded and frustrated.

I have heard some people in hiring positions tell me that caring for kids is the most important thing they are looking for when they are hoping to find a new teacher/educator. As you grow into teaching, seek experiences that remind you of how amazing and wonderful kids can be. Realize that they are going to make many mistakes, even ones you are desperately trying to help them avoid. They are kids. They give us hope, and they will also leave us frustrated. So often they leave us disappointed, but they also leave us amazed.

Working with kids is very difficult. They test your will and emotions at nearly every level. Kids will amaze you beyond your wildest dreams, and they will befuddle you to no end. You can be a good teacher if you love your content, but it will be so much harder to stay in the profession and develop into a master teacher throughout your career if you don't truly care about your kids. For teachers who don't love kids as much, they will find themselves consistently tested by the disappointments, jaded by the students repeated mistakes, and disheartened by the failures - their own and their students'. The biggest part of caring for kids is learning to see the positives they hold. A teacher should be able to say something good about every kid they know. Teachers need to be enriched and empowered by the positives their students provide. If they hope to avoid being jaded and losing their "spark," they will need to be encouraged by small progress and victories for their kids. Great teachers find a way to bask in the warmth of their students' successes, regardless of the grandeur, to re-energize themselves and their teaching.

Be teachable. If caring for kids is the most important quality a teacher should have, being teachable is surely the next best thing. The master educators mentioned in this book have so many things in common, but all of them have a desire and a willingness to learn from others. Each of their stories - their journeys to becoming master educators - includes a history of a willingness to be teachable. Each of them is willing to learn from others, build upon what they know, and accept advice and ideas from others that will make them better as both educators and people.

It can be easy to ignore opportunities to learn, especially as you get deeper into your career. By reading this book, you are already demonstrating that you have some desire to learn more, to question how you can grow, and become a better teacher or person. It shows that you have the desire to learn. You are likely the kind of person who reads, consumes information, and talks with peers in an attempt to grow. But, that impulse can wane over the course of an extended career. Remembering to stay teachable and to accept teachable moments from wherever they present themselves is extremely important for any master educator.

Opportunities to learn can come from anywhere.

Being open to accepting them is a crucial part of being a great educator. There is so much to be learned from peers, administrators, and especially our students if we would only allow ourselves to accept it.

Far too often I hear other educators dismissive of advice they get from administrators. The advice of administrators can sometimes be difficult. They only see a snapshot of your class's learning. At their best, your administrator is piecing together snippets of visits to see how your practice is fitting into their vision for instruction at the school. Yes, they can miss things, but they can also help you learn to put your own reflection into focus. Having an outside observer means that while they don't know what has been happening in your room daily, they also are also removed from it to a degree. This means that they can take a larger perspective about what has happened in the time they are witnessing. Does it necessarily reflect your entire practice? No, of course it doesn't, but it can give you a fresh perspective for you to build your own self-evaluation. Hearing the words of an administrator can often get frustrating, but it is important to accept the learning opportunity and build from it going forward.

We can, as educators, also tend to be dismissive of the lessons our students can provide us. Every day, the kids in our rooms provide us with challenges to overcome and opportunities to learn. Do we turn our back on that? It can be very easy to do so, to be dismissive of or to overlook the lessons our kids teach us.

Being teachable is more than just accepting and

doing what others tell us. It is about learning to take what others offer us, find a way to use it to benefit those with whom we work, and being aware that those offerings might not always be direct.

All these traits live within the incredible master teachers in this book. They not only live there, but they thrive within each. So, the question remains, how do we cultivate these attributes in teachers entering the profession? How are those teachers who choose to embark on a journey toward becoming an educator best equipped to succeed? For different people entering the profession at varied times throughout their lives, the pre-teaching experience may look very different. With that in mind, we need to examine the key attributes that we must foster in new teachers that will help them grow into teachers who excel in the classroom.

Becoming A New Educator

All of us had different pre-teaching or early teaching experiences. As we navigate our way toward education, there is so much to learn. The curve is extremely steep. Unlike in many other professions, teachers are given a relatively short time to build upon their craft before being thrust into the classroom on their own. While classrooms are supposed to be a place of joyous learning, excitement, and wonder, the too often realized possibility of throwing unprepared teachers into the classroom can rob it of the wonder it should contain.

Yet we let most teachers take charge of a classroom without having spent a full year from day one to the last day. Would you let a surgeon perform surgery without ever having been in the operating room for the procedure from beginning to end? Or would you let a lawyer try a case for you if they had never been in the courtroom for a full trial? Absolutely not. I know these aren't exact analogies. There is so much to see and learn about the profession, yet we often throw new teachers into the field without having experienced a complete year in the classroom. We do our pre-service teachers a disservice when we don't give them the opportunity to see a class from beginning to end.

All of us come into teaching with different experiences. Capturing those experiences and teaching our newest educators to find their way depends largely on what the individual needs rather than what we think we should prescribe. Just like teaching any student, we must personalize what our newest educators need to succeed. This means that the professional development of all educators (future and current) should address individual needs. How do we prepare others for this great abyss of independent, personal learning?

First, we ought to be instilling the qualities mentioned above (being curious, humble, reflective, caring, and teachable) into our new teachers. We should be looking for those qualities everywhere, not just teacher candidates for positions, but for candidates for teacher education. Seeking out quality candidates is crucial. Making it more difficult to get into pre-education programs is important. I don't simply mean making the grade and test requirements more stringent. That to me is not nearly as important as learning about the candidates themselves. What kind of people do we want to go into education? Simply put, we want individuals who are caring, teachable, reflective, humble, and curious. Those are the educators who will likely move toward the greatest levels of success in the field and thus have a great impact on the quality of education for the most children. Learn about the candidates from writing samples, interviews, and their past experiences and move on from there.

Once we find the candidates for teacher education, we must then start building in them the ability to learn on their own. They will have so many things to learn during their first few years. Building them into strong learners should be one of the most crucial tasks of any teacher preparation program regardless of who enters.

Pre-Teaching: A Step into the Wild, or Head First into the Deep End?

I didn't have a traditional teacher preparation program. I spent three years as an in-class support aide and long-term sub before landing in my first classroom. As I have stated before, despite spending three years fully immersed in classrooms, it was still incredibly challenging getting started. But, I was able to take all that I had learned and built upon it. It isn't ever going to be easy or straightforward, but becoming a master teacher should be attainable for any teacher starting in a classroom.

Not having the experience of a traditional pre-teaching program, I wanted to know more from teachers whose careers I admired. I also wanted to know more from a professor whose students always seem well-prepared and capable of sharing intelligent thoughts on education. In doing so, I spoke to teachers Sylwia and Rae, both of whom will tell you they are not master teachers. I also spoke to Rider University's Dr. Michael G. Curran, Jr. who has a hand in shaping a number of teachers I have observed as being incredibly well-prepared.

Understanding what makes great learning programs involves the educators who create them, but most importantly the people doing the learning. Getting to learn about the pre-service programs of two teachers who have quickly become excellent at their craft highlighted some important similarities that we should observe.

Great Teacher Education: A Teacher's Perspective

Every time I think of both Sylwia Denko and Rae Hughart I am amazed. These are two teachers who not only survived their first years, but also set themselves up for incredible success early on. Of course, they have dealt with difficulties; their paths have not been smooth at every bend. That said, both have shown an incredible ability to start strong and continue growing throughout the early parts of their careers. In just the fourth year of their careers, there is still so much more for them to experience. There is no doubt in my mind that these two are excellent educators who have so much to teach others.

What helped them walk into the classroom and find more success than survival? There are several common themes in their educational experiences at Rider University in New Jersey and Illinois State University where Sylwia and Rae, respectively, honed their craft.

Sylwia shared with me the great experiences she had at Rider University. She was one of the first students I had the opportunity to connect with while she was still involved in her university experience. Her reflection on the time spent at Rider is a testament both to her dedication and to the University's ability to provide excellent experiences for their students.

"I got to experience so many different classrooms, so many different communities, and so many different grades. By the time I graduated, I was in (classrooms in) six different grades," Sylwia recalls. Rider provided Sylwia with the ability to see inclusion classrooms to gifted and talented classes, early childhood to middle school, and public, private, urban, suburban, and affluent areas. That broad spectrum gave her the ability to gain so many experiences. "What worked was how often I was in the classroom and the diversity of the classrooms I was in," she continued.

Along with the rich and diverse experiences she received in classrooms, Sylwia also had the opportunity to connect with and grow from talking to many educators and leaders around the region. Rider's program included encouraging students to build connections with the teachers in their schools of placement, but also with the guests who came to speak and the network of educators they could begin to build. The combination of an excellent range of experiences, paired with learning how to identify people who could help her grow were important parts of Sylwia's ability to excel early in her career.

Rae's teaching experience at Illinois State University was an incredibly positive one. She chose her undergraduate school because of their education program and their Professional Development Schools (PDS) program. One of the standout features of this program was a part of their teacher preparation program that included a full year of student teaching during her senior year. Some states are moving toward a full-year student teaching program, and there can be significant benefits if done well. "I was able to see the beginning of the year and the end of the year, which is something that I think is lacking in many student teacher programs," Rae says.

Having the ability to see the incredible learning that takes place at both the beginning and the end of the year matters. "If you have only student taught at the end of the year, it is hard to expect someone to start the year off strong the next fall. It is a real disconnect."

Her program provided her with great mentor experiences to combine with continuous opportunities to develop skills in the classroom. "I really needed experience engaging with the students, asking questions, and being able to try things, fail, and try again to ultimately succeed." Her experiences allowed her to gain the practical experiences to connect the classroom and theory work from the program. Having the chance to put ideas into practice, learn and grow with mentors, and see the entire process from beginning to end are all important parts of growth for any new teacher.

Just setting the conditions won't necessarily guarantee success, but when you combine these ideas with dedicated and passionate people, it makes creating a thriving generation of new teachers so much more likely.

While these two amazing educators have slightly different experiences contributing to their early success, both recognize the value of time spent in the classroom and the opportunity to build relationships with mentors. Both point to their being able to interact with students, try out ideas, and work with supportive educators as improving their ability to start their first year well.

The connection between strong, positive, and consistent time spent in classrooms combined with good mentor relationships and success upon entering the classroom is too important to ignore. Part of creating better preparation programs for anyone entering education should include both areas. Seeing how teaching theory applies to real classrooms of varying types, coupled with gaining the experience to navigate difficult situations, has the potential to help any new teacher launch a career that goes beyond survival.

Great Teacher Education: A Professor's Perspective

So then, what aspects help to build a successful program of independent learners as educators? After speaking with Dr. Michael G. Curran of Rider University, the general success of his students and their apparent readiness to enter the classroom seem to hinge on helping students understand how to find what they need and apply it.

Dr. Curran credits the work ethic of the students in his program, but he also sets the conditions for their success. Students are introduced to leading educators in the region who visit his class throughout the semester. They are also required to start building a professional digital presence. They need to post to Twitter at least ten times a week referencing meaningful education and technology articles or resources. During that time, Dr. Curran encourages them to build connections with other educators. The seeds of great mentor relationships are sown by developing connections for these early educators.

Perhaps the most important thing Dr. Curran expects his students to do is to spend 30 minutes of every day on professional development. It builds into new educators the importance of being curious, of being teachable, and being reflective. By spending 30 minutes every day focusing on learning for themselves, new educators are given the opportunity and support to become independent learners.

While that half hour may not always apply to whatever they are going to do in their future classrooms, it does prime them for the great challenges ahead. Pre-teaching experiences should not just be about learning to teach (that still needs to be a big part of it), but if we are going to set up our next generations for success, they must also acquire these critical skills of learning, cultivating beneficial relationships, and of sharing learning with one another. Dr. Curran and the staff at Rider University do a phenomenal job of giving their future teachers the tools they need to become master teachers.

I am sure there are plenty of teachers that fit Sylwia's and Rae's paths toward being incredible teachers. But, from everyone I have seen and spoken with, it is not the norm. There are also many great education departments around the world that are working to create better experiences for potential teachers. As a community of educators, we should be looking for ways to try and help expand on those successes, and create more teachers that enter the profession with the ability to do more than simply survive in their early years.

Finding Our Way: Searching for Guides

Our first time in the classroom can be

intimidating, overwhelming, and exhilarating all at once. Learning to navigate the pre-teaching classroom experience can be difficult for many reasons. It is rare that developing teachers find great matches to work with them in the classroom. Who accepts these young hopefuls into their classroom? New teachers have fewer alternatives with the current evaluation systems because potential mentor teachers are less likely to take the risk of adding an unknown element into their craft.

Minnesota is just one state experiencing this trouble. "Some of the state's most highly skilled veteran teachers are reluctant to take on the extra responsibility of hosting a student teacher when they have been asked to do other demanding new tasks such as serving as peer evaluators" (McGuire, 2015). I have heard many teachers and pre-service teachers share these concerns. So many teachers I have spoken to regarding welcoming the next generation do so for one of two reasons either earning a stipend, or a deep commitment to helping new teachers. If you find yourself with the second type, you are extremely fortunate. If not, you will find yourself in survival mode before you even start your career.

What do aspiring teachers need and want out of this experience? After talking with a group of pre-service and newer teachers about mentoring and growth in their pre-service teaching experience, some of the greatest frustrations were in trying to work with others who provided them with no guidance. Young teachers working in a pre-service classroom experience are frustrated. Some teachers were overwhelmed by a complete lack of support or gradual integration by their cooperating teacher. Others were simply not allowed to take over any aspects of the classroom for more than half a semester. Neither of these will do.

Just as any visitor to my classroom, in the past I have expected an observing teacher to take an active role in the room. That role includes engaging with and helping kids whenever possible. For potential educators, I also required some debriefing time at the end of the day. I wanted them to talk about what they saw, what they noticed with themselves, with the students, and with me. This debriefing process makes us both better.

All the teachers I spoke with were looking for a partner in their learning process. They visit many classrooms throughout their journey toward becoming an educator, and in each one, they need to find a partner who is willing to invest some time in their development.

Whether you go through a traditional program or some alternative path, finding these early guides can have a major effect on the type of educator you become. It also has a dramatic impact on your ability to survive the trials of your early career. What I find most concerning, however, is the inability of those young educators to identify those partners on their own and build lasting relationships with them. We must empower them to find those mentors beyond the classroom they are assigned. By learning about and from more people in the schools in which they are assigned, they can start to develop better mentor relationships.

This has been my continual parting advice for new educators, and educators in general: collect good people. Continue to find and build relationships with those good people, and call upon them whenever you need to do so. Being a developing teacher, or any teacher for that matter is difficult. Doing so alone is unnecessary and makes the journey more arduous.

Part of finding your people is to build and maintain the connections with good people along the way. I have found only a few new teachers who continue to build connections with the educators they meet. This needs to be stressed at every level of education so that teachers can learn and grow throughout their careers. Having others to work with, to turn to for help with teaching and with life, is an important tool that we can give teachers to do more than simply survive their journey through this profession.

The Alternate Pre-Teaching Experience

As we have seen through our various Teacher Heroes, not all of us come to the classroom through the traditional route. So many teachers come to the classroom with varying experiences that are far different from those provided by traditional teacher education programs. While we can hopefully influence teacher education programs, the experience of teachers that migrate to education after their initial undergraduate education is more of a wildcard. While I can point to numerous examples of educators that are incredibly impactful that come from the two less traditional archetypes, the fact remains that working toward education after college has a lot more variables toward success.

Like Victor Small, Jr., I decided to teach after spending time as a school substitute. Although I was not prepared well enough, one of the things that helped prepare me for starting as an educator was the time I spent in classrooms working with kids and excellent educators. I spent three full years in the school district and two years where I worked with the same class from start to finish. So much of what I learned was in practice and from talking to the supportive people around me.

When I switched districts to take my first job, I lost touch with those people, and in losing touch, lost an important factor that helped me learn to be an educator. While I did have some formal teaching education, it was a graduate level program. It didn't deal with teaching basics, but instead focused on higher level ideas. At the time, it seemed to be the best choice. In retrospect, however, it might not have prepared me as well as I would have hoped, regarding the theoretical teaching ideas that I was putting into practice in the classroom. Those are ideas I would learn later as I developed into a better educator.

Stephanie Filardo dealt with a very common struggle leading up to her first year in the classroom: getting the opportunity to get into the classroom. She spent time working as a sub to build experience and relationships. During that time, she wrote to BrainPOP to share her positive experiences with the tool during her student teaching. Through reaching out to BrainPOP, she developed a mentoring relationship with Kari Stubbs who set her up with some opportunities to work with them. "I am a conference junkie, and without that experience, none of the things I had done since then (professionally) would have happened. If I had actually gotten a job to work that August, I don't think I would have been able to do the things I have [done]."

Working in classrooms, taking classes, and doing another full-time job is a difficult way to get into teaching. It does, however, provide potential advantages for the working teacher who has an increased ability to build connections between both his class and content, and between other educators. When Jon Corippo moved to the classroom on April 1st, he had almost no training. His experiences in the class weren't a joke. He was thrown into the alternative certification program as a long-term sub. After several months of work, he attended his first class. "I was hooked after about three days," Jon remembered as he reflected upon his first experiences in the classroom.

Jon built his career while working on an emergency credential program. He was able to continue building that career, but what was it that made him successful? Jon had experience as a football coach and in working to teach adults how to use technology. Those experiences certainly helped. Having entered the classroom from another career without the benefit of ever spending significant time in the classroom is challenging.

Jon has demonstrated throughout his career that he is exceptional. In this case, Jon's success is in part due to his ability to adapt, learn, and inspire others. Not everyone has the ability to transition successfully to another career.

Teachers coming to the profession through an alternate route still need the right support if they are going to be successful. We do, however, have some things in common with those who come from more traditional programs. We tend to gain knowledge from having meaningful classroom experiences. Whether we achieve this through working in the classroom as a support teacher or being thrown into the fire from day one, learning to teach through actually teaching is important. What we typically don't see with so many of these teachers is the supplement of teaching theory as it is applied to their practice.

Alternate programs tend to give you the bare bones. In alternative teaching programs, lesson planning and basic management tend to dominate the curriculum. Instead, these pre-service teachers should be learning to balance the theory that their peers get in college with the experiences they have gained in teaching. They also need to have good mentors (as we all do) to help guide them through the most difficult parts of their early career.

When I came to my classroom, I had an idea of

what I wanted to be as a teacher. I wanted to be like Dawn, who was the first teacher who really adopted me as a project and decided to help me learn. That only took me so far. I had no idea how to make myself a better teacher for most of my first two years. I was getting better by chance rather than intentionally improving things that I needed to make better. I knew what wasn't working, and I could make small changes to fix small problems, but to become a great teacher was something that wasn't within sight.

By my third year, I had started to figure out how to make more things work. I had built confidence and an understanding of the curriculum, the community, and the staff with whom I worked. What I still lacked was an understanding of how to be intentional, how to find others to help me, and how to use my classroom experiences combined with new learning to make my classroom a better place to learn. Teachers who find themselves surrounded by good people, and who learn how to reflect on their classroom experiences to understand becoming a better teacher are the ones who will be successful, no matter what the entry point.

The Next Step

While there are many ways we could approach and reflect on how we grow new teachers, let's focus on you right now. After all, this is about YOUR journey. So, whether you were student teaching 30 years ago or you are still waiting for your first chance to take the responsibility in a classroom, spend a few minutes reflecting on how your abilities can make a difference.

Pre-Service Teachers

1. Start thinking now; how can I be proactive in my on-site learning? You will be placed in a classroom, and in many ways, the rest is up to you. While you may not always get a great cooperating teacher, you can take it upon yourself to learn as much as possible. Take time to meet with other teachers as well.

2. Who have you met so far in education who can help you? How can you keep in touch with them? One of the most important things you can do is to start making connections with the educators you meet along the way.

3. What can you do to start directing your own learning? Find books, find blogs, find people who can make a difference in your education to become a teacher.

New Teachers

1. If you have an opportunity, try to find a way to give back to your college community by offering to share your experiences as a new teacher with students.

2. Keep the connections between yourself and the people you learned from during

your pre-service years. Reach out to them just to say hi and let them know how your year is going. Chances are, you will need help, and they can be an excellent resource.

Junior Teachers

1. Pre-service teachers looking to get into the profession should be right up your alley. There is no better way to improve your own teaching than to work on teaching it to someone else. You may think, "I am not ready for that responsibility." The reality is, if not you, then who?

2. Think about the things you love to share with others. Find ways to share them with pre-service teachers, whether through online resources or in-person visits. Need an extra hand? See if any local colleges have any pre-service teachers who want to volunteer.

Master Teachers

When you have been giving back to the teaching community, you will undoubtedly have spent time working with pre-service teachers in some capacity. While I encourage you to take on more responsibilities with developing educators including preservice teachers, you should also consider other paths.

1. Help anyone who is going to have a pre-service teacher in their classroom. Work with them on helping teachers be reflective and helping them develop relationships outside of their classroom.
2. Reach out to any pre-service teachers in your building. Find out who they are and start helping them make connections to with yourself and with other good people in education.

Chapter 5

A Strange New World: Entering the Classroom

Why Aren't Teachers Ready for Day One?

I have heard teachers say, "theory goes out the window the moment you get in the classroom." Why? If that is the case, what's wrong with the theory? In truth, I remember almost nothing from my teaching classes. That isn't to say that I haven't incorporated things I learned, but rather that none of it stands out. What does stand out is three years of experience in classrooms before I started teaching. Without those years, those experiences, and those guides who helped me along the way, I would not have seen beyond my first year, or perhaps my first week.

Despite my practical understanding and development, there were many times during my first few years of teaching that I felt horribly unprepared because of jargon and unfamiliar acronyms. I can recall sitting in an interview for my first teaching job and being asked about Universal Design for Learning (UDL). I said I didn't know what it was, then went on to describe practices that exemplified it. From my practical experiences, I knew how to do some things, just not what they were called.

As you've already read, my first year was a major

challenge. I learned a great deal before walking into the classroom, but this was different. Despite having some incredible experiences before becoming a teacher, I couldn't have imagined the things that I needed to learn and discover in that first year. When the door shut on the first day, I was responsible. These kids would either learn or not, succeed or not, based on what I did. There was a pressure that hadn't been there before. I was officially in over my head. Not really, but when I looked out over my class for the first time, I certainly felt that way.

In retrospect, I was extremely well prepared. At the moment, I felt naked, exposed for the fraud I was, who had talked himself into a job despite having no idea what I was doing. Have you ever felt like this? It seems like first-year teaching is often this bizarre blend of incredible learning experiences, mixed with the horror that others might find out you don't know what you are doing. When I finally thought I'd made it, that I had been successful in becoming a teacher, my first day got exciting.

On this day, I had a five-year-old girl explain to the eighth-grader accompanying her, that she rode a different bus than the one she was being put on. Our youngest students were always walked to the bus by our 8th-grade safeties. In this case, a young teenager who responsible for getting a small child from the classroom to her bus, allowed a five-year-old child be the sole voice of that decision. My student was on the wrong bus. I had lost a student without knowing it. Not only was it my student, but it was also the head of the

Home School Association's child. This was my worst nightmare.

For nearly an hour, I waited with our Chief School Administrator and the girl's understandably irate parents for the bus she had mistakenly boarded to arrive back at school. A rousing start to my new career.

There have been many downturns in my career. I share these with you for two reasons. One, the idea that any of us is perfect or without struggle is absurd. Two, when we overcome these difficulties, they become a crucial part of our journey.

While the difficulties are an important part of the journey, we ought to do more to aid ourselves and other Teacher Heroes along the way. What advice do we give our fellow teachers as they embark on new endeavors? I have heard others say many things: stay out of the teachers' lounge, don't tell kids about yourself, keep your head down and close your door. These are just a few popular sayings, often passed off as advice for teachers entering the profession. You undoubtedly heard at least one of these in your career. They lack merit.

I, admittedly, did two of these three things in my first year. I almost never went in the lounge, and I absolutely closed my door and kept my head down. Where did it leave me? It left me alone and anxious that others would think I didn't know what I was doing.

The first piece of advice about staying clear of the teacher's lounge is one I stuck with for a while. It isn't the best place at times. The private sanctuary of teachers often can turn into a toxic vent. So why go in there? Simple. You need to get to know the people around you. For better or worse, these are your coworkers. I learned a lot about who I would choose to trust, who I wanted to collaborate with (if given the choice), and over time, how and when to best advocate for my students. In that first year, I almost never went to the lounge. I still felt a bit like an outsider, despite the generally welcoming attitude others had shown. Over time, I went in more and listened. I learned about the people around me and shared a little with them about my life.

You need to collect the good people in your building.

As much as I will continue to stress the value of branching out beyond your local area to find your mentors, having mentors in your building makes a difference. There are times in your career when you need someone...someone right then and there who knows the situations you are talking about and can guide you. Someone who can listen without judging and help you navigate difficult situations. In the past several years of my career, I have made it a point to find those people and develop those relationships. They have been invaluable to my career and my sanity.

What do I look for in those people? They don't need to teach like I teach, they simply need to fit three basic standards:

1. They genuinely care about kids.
2. They aren't constantly talking negatively

about others (everyone has a bad day, but if you see someone who does this every day they are not great to be around).
3. When you tell them something, they don't turn the focus around to themselves.

This is what I look for in finding good people in my building. There are other things I appreciate, but these are requirements. If you cannot find one person who fits this mold within a few months, you may want to start looking for another teaching opportunity.

So, go in the lounge. Go in and listen. Be aware you will hear some negativity. In time, you will hopefully learn to combat that negativity.

By my third year and throughout the rest of my career to date, I can recall plenty of times when I shut down negative conversations. As you start doing it, others will too. If you are still new, I would suggest treading lightly. Pick your battles. As you establish yourself in the school, you will understand its politics. Part of creating positive change is working to change negative narratives that can exist behind closed doors. You will learn a great deal about your colleagues from listening.

Ok, go in the lounge. But, what about closing your door and keeping your head down? Isn't it the best way to survive each day? Maybe not. Do you really just want to *survive* this journey? Is it good enough to just go unnoticed? There will undoubtedly be some who are happy just to exist and get by. If that is you, perhaps you can think back to a time when this wasn't the case.

Chances are if you are reading this book, getting by isn't typically enough for you.

What happens when you close your doors and shut yourself in? You end up alone.

My first year was spent locked away in my room. I rarely left during the school day. I absolutely advocate for making meaningful use of your time, eating with kids, and putting effort into your work. What I also advocate for is avoiding isolation, sharing what you know, and learning from others. It is hard to do any of those by simply closing your door.

Like myself, Victor Small, Jr. was given the adage, "Never let them see you smile until November." This is part of the bigger concept of not letting them see you as a person.

Along with this, Sarah Thomas was told she needed to dress in extremely formal business attire to ensure the students would respect her. This idea that we need to set ourselves apart from students and force them to see us as somehow inhuman, or to respect our authority goes against everything I have since learned in my career about building relationships with kids.

I couldn't skip telling my students about myself. In truth, it is what they care most about. They want to know about you and your life. While I do find dressing professionally important to maintaining that teaching is a profession, I also like for kids to see me in "regular clothes" to remind them that I am also a regular person. In the end, what you choose to wear is a personal choice, but building good relationships is not. Smiling, sharing about yourself, and asking kids about themselves are all important to build the relationships that allow us to reach them in areas that go beyond content.

I owe a tremendous amount to two individuals who saw potential in me. Those two mentors were my first principal, Sherry Bosch, and the first teacher I worked with on a long-term basis, Dawn Skomsky, and they gave me guidance. They shared their knowledge and philosophy with me. Most importantly they gave me trust. Both gave me the trust of working with their students. Some might think of this as a small thing. But, for these educators who took the lives of their students to heart, trusting a young, inexperienced hopeful with their students, that trust was a huge deal.

The eighteen months I worked with Dawn and the following year where I student taught and finished the year as an aide gave me as much preparation as possible. I had experienced nearly everything (I thought) that a teacher could, and had done so with quality. It was time.

Leaving the school where I started was difficult, but I think it made me a better teacher. By day one, I was ready...until I wasn't. It wasn't that I saw too many "new" things in my first year, it was that I was responsible for making sure my kids were successful. When the train would derail, it was my job to find the tracks again. When the buck stops with you, it changes your perspective.

Therein lies one of the major differences in the entire process: responsibility. You can teach lessons, talk with families, work with administrators, and learn from other teachers during your preparation period, but there is a huge difference when you are ultimately responsible. There are other differences as well. It is easy to miss these things during teacher preparation, or even when you are eagerly trying to impress with the hopes of getting a job.

Responsibility

I walked across the library toward a familiar face. One of my student's parents had spoken out in support of our teachers, during what had been an incredibly contentious board meeting thus far. All our teaching staff was there. I wanted to thank her for her kind words and for offering her support. It was during that conversation I learned what my class had meant to her and her son.

He was a sweet little boy who was kind, caring, and easy to like. I always saw him as friendly and hardworking. Despite having a good relationship with him, I had no idea what he was going through outside of my classroom (which can often be the case). As it turns out, it was in my classroom where he felt safe, valued, and at ease with himself. He felt like he could talk to me about things and be himself. I had just assumed he was like that everywhere, but as it turns out, he wasn't. With tear-filled eyes, his mother thanked me for being kind and supportive, and inspiring her son to want to learn new things. I spent the rest of that night with tingles that still come back as I think about it.

Several times a year I get Facebook messages from parents or see them (or their children) out in public where they remind me of the impact I have had on their lives. I could share dozens of stories that exemplify the impact I have had, as could many teachers. Despite the many positive stories, there are always kids that I worry about.

There are always kids that I wish I could have done more to reach. That is the weight of being an educator, we want to reach them all, and for many, you never get to find out if you made an impact.

If that burden weighs on you as it does many educators, I can guarantee you are making a much larger impact than you think. Had I never taken the time to thank that mother, had she not stood up to speak at our board meeting, I might never have known how much my class meant to her family. That moment exemplifies one of my favorite TED Talks, *Drew Dudley's Everyday Leadership or Lollipop Moments*.[2]

Dudley tells the story of a girl who claims to have had her whole life changed by one silly moment of interaction with a complete stranger over four years earlier. How often do we tell the people who have changed our lives how much they mean to us? It is so easy to let these moments in our lives pass by without action. "And if you change one person's understanding

---

[2] https://www.ted.com/talks/drew_dudley_everyday_leadership

of it, understanding of what they're capable of, understanding of how much people care about them, understanding of how powerful an agent for change they can be in this world, you've changed the whole thing" (Dudley, 2010).

So many educators never hear the great impact they have had on the lives of others, yet their impact can be profound. No one may have told you, but I promise you, you have changed the world.

We have an incredible ability as educators to create a ground level impact on the world. You, yes, *you*, the educator reading this book, can change the whole world through your interactions with one child. You may never know what you've done. You may find out years later, or perhaps that same day. Sometimes it takes the worst circumstances to know how you've changed a life.

Those stories ought to stick with you, and they often do. They aren't the glamour of teaching, they are the heart. As an educator, what I have done with my life is not measured in proficiency, but in lives changed. This is my greatest responsibility.

What are the things we do every day that make this happen? How can we change the world? We change the world with our actions.

Something changed for me the moment the door shut on that first day. It is a feeling that never fully goes away. That feeling is the same one that keeps me excited for each new school year: when the door closes, and the heart of teaching really begins. This is your chance to create new relationships, teach kids new things, and have a real impact on the lives of others.

While that is an amazing thing, it is also terrifying. What I do with these kids in front of me could potentially change their lives. As a teacher in the profession for over ten years, that prospect is still what fuels me (along with coffee) to bring my best to the classroom each day.

As an educator, I have many responsibilities. There are the glamorous ones as I mentioned, and the not-so-glamorous ones that involve paperwork or meetings about things unrelated to kids. There aren't books or movies about these responsibilities. In all fairness, they would be pretty boring books. Can you imagine a book where the caption was, "Follow the heroic Mrs. B while she fills out reports, administers state testing, and meets state-mandated professional development requirements!" That book would fly off the shelves!

The truth is, however, if you don't learn systems to manage these more mundane responsibilities, they start to take away from your ability to handle the responsibilities that are most important. For me, this was one of the hardest things to learn as a young teacher. Personally, I care much less about most of that stuff. Regardless of personal feelings, it still must be done well.

How do you manage the less exciting tasks like paperwork? In truth, it comes down to personal choice. Like most students, I was a procrastinator. I finished things in the early morning hours before they were due and pretended I "worked best under pressure." If you live your teaching life that way, you will find yourself treading water and struggling to avoid burnout. So, here are some ideas for dealing with the hundreds of things you need to accomplish each day:

1. You will have seemingly excessive paperwork. Know your schedule. It sounds so simple, but plan for specific times to get paperwork finished. Work on it with a friend, coach, or mentor. Also, don't just plan one time, plan two or three. If you finish in one session, you get found time. Found time for teachers is like the 20-dollar bill in your winter coat: it was always yours, you just didn't realize it!

2. Create a functional template for your lesson plans. Prewrite as much of it as possible, so you only have to change the things that are happening on an individual day. It sounds silly, but lesson plans can eat up a ton of time. (I am not talking about actually planning lessons, but the writing of lesson plans.)

3. Come up with a system of organization for your paperwork. Whether you are like me and you need to digitize everything and keep it online, or you are legendary with binders, knowing what and where important documents are can be a huge

time-saver.

4. Start thinking about your future. Start to create a long-term planning guide for yourself that includes personal, professional, and educational goals. Identify who can help you achieve those goals.

Political Landscape

School is a weird place. You rarely see it as a kid going through the system. It may have something to do with the social nature of school, or perhaps it happens in many professional workplaces, but rarely are new teachers ready for it. Understanding the crazy political landscape that breathes within most school buildings will allow new teachers to improve in their first years, and allow master teachers to really begin making positive changes in the school.

I never truly understood the political landscape of a school until I began studying to be an administrator. This was still early in my career. I had not yet started my fourth year. Our first reading assignment was a book called *Reframing the Path to School Leadership* (Bolman & Deal, 2010). I have reread it several times. It is one of many good books, but it alerted me to my own naivete in my surroundings. I had always assumed school was a special place where politics didn't really enter the equation. Having studied political science in college, I realized I had no interest in politics. What I never fully understood was how every workplace has its own unique political landscape.

I found politics to be a major issue in the school after nearly three years of ignorant bliss (about these politics). You may laugh, or you may relate. For nearly two years, I had managed to remain absurdly unaware of the various players in the political game within my school. Even after some of it was unveiled, I still understood so little of how the players in my school impacted what happened there. You may know how this works, but it was new to me.

Nearly three years into my career, I had managed to run afoul of someone in my district. She was strong-willed, loud, and used that combination to complain about everything from teachers to parents to kids. I didn't know her well, especially considering I had just started to venture out of my room by the middle of year two. I did, however, interact with her because she was teaching some of my former students.

Near the end of that year, I was working out with another teacher after school. We had become friendly and started doing workouts after school. I had made a paperwork mistake on cumulative folders. (If you don't know what they are, I hope you don't need to learn.) It was during my second year, and I was filling them out for a new grade level, whose procedure was different from the way I'd done it before. Take this lesson from me, always ask with paperwork...don't guess.

When the loud teacher confronted me about my mistakes, I was on my way to start working out. I had finished for the day. She accused me of not doing my job and told me that I needed to do it. I said I would, and just walked away.

The next morning there was a pile of folders on my desk (I still had a desk then). On top of the folders was a note from my CSA (Chief School Administrator) saying that I needed to complete the back paperwork as soon as possible. What happened? I didn't understand how I could have gone from saying I would do something, to having my boss write me a note directing me to drop everything and do this work.

What happened was that this loud teacher decided to make a big deal about it because I had inconvenienced her. She ranted to other teachers, including some I had become friendly with during that year. She also ranted to the CSA, leaving out all the actual details. Her political power in the school had put me in a compromising position.

How does one handle a situation like this? Do so cordially and professionally, but directly. I am not a huge fan of direct confrontations. I don't usually speak before I think; I prefer to allow my emotions to cool and think through situations logically. That was exactly what helped me navigate this mess.

I crafted an email to the teacher and CCed it to the CSA. I let her know that I didn't appreciate the lack of professional courtesy regarding her remarks to other staff members about an issue between us. I also mentioned how it was unnecessary for her to report the situation to an administrator, because I had told her I would take care of it quickly. I did not have a single work minute to complete the tasks and correct mistakes she had brought to my attention before it was reported. Her response was short and made little sense.

The next morning our CSA pulled me into her office. This was when I realized how this person's political power in the school, as well as her negative effect on the culture at the school, had been so significant. The CSA thanked me for standing up to her. She asked me to continue to do so whenever necessary, and that I should quietly encourage more people to shut down the excessive negativity she brought.

I had assumed I was in trouble; instead, I found I had built some serious political capital with a lot of the staff members who were tired of that voice taking up more space in the room than it needed. I had also built more capital with my CSA.

Politics in schools can be a funny thing. They tend to be less overt, but if you don't notice them, they can undermine everything you hope to do. Knowing the people who hold sway over certain groups can be the difference between making real change and having an idea or initiative shut down. School is (often quietly) one of the most political places you will find. You will find power dynamics across the major stakeholders in education. Companies, governments, school boards, teachers, parents, administrators, and more, all have a voice in what happens in a school.

Some of you are thinking, "not my school... nope,

everyone gets along here. There's no politics happening here." First let me apologize because once you learn it, you won't be able to unsee it. Then, let me allow you the opportunity to let this sink in...

Your school is a vast, subtle, yet wildly diverse political landscape. You may not see it, but it is there. Each stakeholder has his or her own beliefs and fits into the power dynamic within the school or district. This isn't to say that is a bad thing. It is simply part of the reality. Understanding that reality will allow you to create meaningful shifts in your school. When you know who the players are, then you can start building your support.

Less than three years ago I was hoping to start a makerspace in my school. I had found another teacher who knew what I was talking about and was seriously interested. Meghan was newer to teaching and had only been there a few months, but she also knew what a makerspace was and that was a start. On one of the last days of school, we talked about it for the first time.

After the last day was over, we approached our CSA (a different one than the previous story in this section). We asked him if we could use a portion of the library that wasn't being used to create a makerspace. We gave him a brief description of our rough vision, and we showed him the space we wanted. He simply asked, "What will it cost?" to which we replied, "nothing."

That was good enough to let him say ok, but not enough to make the space an established part of the school. He was intrigued, but we needed to make it something that could not go away. We wanted to build a culture that embraced this mentality in the classrooms and beyond.

Our first step was the kids. When the space opened, kids had already heard plenty about what would be there. We had kids waiting to enter every day.

Next, we needed to build support from other groups. We tried professional development with our staff, but it didn't go too far. They loved the space, but weren't likely to bring kids there for lessons: failure one.

We decided to try a different route. We wanted to convince the school board (who held board meetings in plain sight of our space) and a key group of parents that ran the Home School Association, and nearly all the fundraising and events in the school.

We presented how we built our space and why we need makerspaces and maker culture in our school. It was received with remarkable excitement. The board loved how we were giving kids hands-on experiences and encouraging creativity. The parents loved those things as well, but even more, they loved how much their own kids loved the space. (Ironic side note to this: the school board was also interviewing people to fill a vacancy. Right after our presentation, they interviewed a person who said, "I don't believe in computers." To this day, I still find it hilarious that we won the room talking about robots, circuits, and computers right before he gave that answer.)

We had just won two major stakeholders in the School Board and the Home School Association (HSA).

A Strange New World: Entering the Classroom

We got funding for several projects from the HSA, and were able to bring in guests to teach our students more about the technology they were finding. We also found ways to get significantly more materials donated from parents in the community. By the end of the year, we had secured a budget for the makerspace. It was officially going to be part of the school's budget.

Schools are political places. They are not free from the pulls and prods of the powerful hoping to assert their ideals upon the rest. Politics are in education, regardless, on a macro level at the federal, state, and school board levels, to a micro level within the school itself. Either you acknowledge them and learn to use them for yourself, or they will use you.

If you want to have a broader impact on your school, you must recognize the influencers. Who can help or hinder what you hope to accomplish? How can you get them on your side? What are the consequences, both good and bad of gaining support or opposing a certain group? Is your compromise with each group worth it to accomplish your goal? Stakeholders are important. They need to be heard, but they also need to be respected for their ability to either make your work successful or stop you in your tracks.

Ebbs and Flows

A school year is not a sprint, it is more like an ultramarathon. I can't say I have ever run an ultramarathon, but I can imagine it being a combination of physical and mental strength, endurance, and filled with challenges and euphoria.

The year will, at times, go by so quickly that it seems like time disappeared, and other times your days may seem to drag. How can it only be Thursday? Yes, those days happen to the best of us. The challenge is how we stay focused during those times. What can you do to slow yourself down when the year is flying by? How can you strengthen your resolve and continue to be a positive influence on kids during the days and weeks when things seem to drag? Those are important questions at any stage of your journey.

Right now, you are probably thinking, "Why do I need to slow down during those great times when everything is going well, and it's all moving by so quickly?" If you are not new to this journey, then you have undoubtedly entered a year with the best intentions of trying something you are really excited about. It may have been a cool project, a new activity, or something that would have really pushed you outside of your comfort zone. Those things are what can create a great experience during the year for both you and your kids.

A lot of times when it all flows so quickly, it is because you have hit a good rhythm. I am not suggesting that you disrupt the rhythm, but instead to evaluate where you are at a given time and look at where you started. This type of reflective activity can be incredibly helpful to avoid your path becoming a runaway train. While you want to experience that rhythm, you also want to make sure you are not on autopilot. Using reflection helps.

Whether you write, record video, or talk with someone, going through your experiences and seeing how they match up to your expectations can be an incredible learning opportunity. It also creates a strong sense of who you are as an educator and who you would like to be. I enjoy writing, so I tend to blog.

At one point, I was writing daily posts to reflect on whatever struck me that day. It was a very powerful reflection tool. I have gotten away from a daily blog, but do post at a minimum of once a week, sometimes more. I know others who keep journals, or vlogs (video blogs), or who simply meet with a mentor once a week for coffee to talk out their experiences. No matter how you choose to reflect on what you have done, the act of thinking critically about what you've done is crucial to improving.

This can also help with the times of struggle as well. We cannot always be perfect. We cannot always have the full burst of positive energy we want. You will certainly experience days where you are the frustrated teacher from all the internet memes talking about how wine should be your holiday gift.

So, what then? Well, reflection helps. Learning to celebrate your small victories daily helps as well. Look at what is going on in your class. Hit the reset button if you need to, but think about what you had planned on happening and what is actually happening.

What isn't working? What is in your control to change? Is there someone who can help you make your original vision happen? These are some of the reflective questions that might help you move forward when things are most difficult. Ask them of yourself, think honestly about the answers, then make the changes you need to make to get your classroom where you want it to be.

You will undoubtedly go through highs and lows. There are times that you settle into an incredible groove and teaching comes so naturally, you think you've got it covered. There are other times, however, where things get choppy; where the path through that year is unclear, unkempt, or seemingly unmanageable. How we make the most of the times that flow beautifully and how we push through the rough patches during a year can impact our ability to help kids, and also our teacher's journey overall.

The P Word: Parents

"How do you deal with parents?"

"This job would be great if I didn't have to deal with parents all the time."

"Why can't his/her parents just do what they are supposed to do?"

You either have heard or will hear these questions from the mouths of some teachers in your school. Don't attempt to answer them. They aren't legitimate questions.

Parents aren't people you deal with, nor are they the reason for your job being difficult. Your job is difficult because you make 25,000 decisions a day where each one creates a ripple effect on an entire group, not just a single person in the room. Those decisions can either create a positive change in the way your kids experience learning in the world, or they can undermine it. Parents are key allies in creating a classroom where teachers can build a better environment for kids to learn. Remember when I said that schools are political? Parents are a driving factor in that equation. You want them as allies. But how?

Let's start by rephrasing the first question. "How do you deal with parents?" I don't "deal" with them. We aren't exchanging goods or services, and they aren't some burden on me. I work with parents. "How might you work with parents?" Now there is a question we can build on to create partners in our parents.

In my first year of teaching, I was 25. I was sitting with a parent who was perhaps only slightly older than I was, having a parent-teacher conference. We talked about what was happening with her child in my class. It was at that point when I realized how much parents need us, and we need them. The whole "school" thing works so much better when we work together. She asked me for parenting advice. I was still a kid. I had barely even taught my own class for three months, I had no children of my own, and yet she was asking for my help. Why? Because parenting is hard.

The reality is that parents can be frustrating at times. I learned a lot about working with parents after becoming a parent. That doesn't mean that every teacher needs to be a parent to be successful. In fact, I still held many of these beliefs before being a parent; the change was more in my ability to understand parenting struggles on a new level. If you are a parent, you will undoubtedly understand these points. If you are not, be open, listen, and think about your experiences with parents to date.

Parenting is incredibly hard. Kids do things for you in school that they would never do for parents, and many times the reverse is true. If you are a parent, you know that it can be difficult to you get your child to go to bed, eat the right foods, or accomplish whatever specific tasks you are hoping they finish. For most of us, the simple act of getting a child to put their shoes on to get out the door can be more challenging than designing vehicles for interstellar travel.

I, and other educators, have expressed how difficult raising children can be, and yet we expect excellence from the parents in our classes who are typically without training in child development or experiences in early childhood learning.

So, start by remembering that first. Parenting is hard. Then remember this: most parents love their children and want what is best for them. Yes, you will certainly encounter a few outliers. They are not the norm. Even kids whose parents seem to be the most careless with their responsibilities typically still really love their kids.

People can, at times, have too many difficulties in their lives for them to really handle them well and still be as awesome as that Pinterest mom you follow. At times they need help...not a savior, but someone who they can partner with to help their kids on multiple fronts. But how? How do might you really work with parents as a partner?

It starts with empathy, or at least understanding that being a parent is really challenging and that parents love their kids. As Kory Graham states, "Most parents really care about and want what's best for their child. What that looks like or how they think that is possible, might not match up to what you think that looks like. This parent loves their child." Start from that place when you approach conversations with parents. From there you have a few important jobs as the educator if you are going to forge meaningful alliances with parents.

First, be a listener. Parents send what is the most important and meaningful thing in their lives off to a place with so many unknowns. They send us their babies, and they do this with the hope that this place is going to help them learn, grow, and become better as a person. Many parents, however, didn't have a personal experience of school as a positive place. You are their point of contact to ensure that their child does. Listen to their concerns. REALLY listen. They may be completely unwarranted, but they stem from something. If you are going to understand more about the lives of your children and forge any positive alliance with your students' families going forward, you will need to listen to their needs, fears, and concerns.

Next, be honest when you talk with parents. Obviously, you need to be aware of what you can and cannot (legally) say, but just as you build meaningful relationships with both students and other educators, you are also building those relationships with parents.

Parents appreciate your being honest with them. When I say that, I don't mean brutal, tactless honesty, but honesty nonetheless. Every time I speak with parents about their children I interact with a sense of honesty. That honesty is focused on solving problems. How might we make this better? What does your child do well?

Make sure you talk to parents about positive things. Again, this isn't a means to sugarcoat your message, but imagine discussing your teaching with an administrator and they only discussed what you struggled to do. If you sat in that meeting for ten minutes and only heard negatives about your performance, how soon would you tune that person out? How can you talk about someone for ten minutes and only have negative things to say? No matter what it is, you can find something positive to say about a child.

Invite parents in. Do it openly. So many teachers will complain about parent visitation days. They are looking at it all wrong. If a parent wants to come into my classroom (and this happened at times), they were treated as I would any volunteer. They were a part of the room that day. It might mean I ask them to do something with a group of students, help with an activity, or get something we need. Parents need positive experiences in schools as well. Twice a year, I used to invite all the parents and extended families into our class. Anytime you plan an important event, try to give four to six weeks' notice. Not every parent can just take time off to come to your event at school, no matter how much they love their child.

Days when parents are invited to the school offer a chance for their children to show what they have learned, and a chance to eat, laugh, and socialize. It was a chance for me to have low pressure, positive conversations with parents. There is nothing to build the positive connection with parents like a fun, welcoming event. Was it difficult? Of course. Organizing an event that included 40-50 kids, teachers, and family members is a challenge. It can be stressful, but the benefits are outstanding for your relationships with parents.

Finally, let them vent. There will be times when you are the target of their frustration. It is often not about you. Don't take it personally.

I can recall a specific phone call where a father spent several minutes yelling at me about Pokémon cards. It was full of anger about overstepping my place, infringing on his kid's rights, but the real part of it was that he didn't want to have things that were for his house go to the child's mother's house. After hearing him yell (he needed to get it out), I suggested a solution to the problem, and he agreed.

Afterward, my CSA had told me not to take that abuse. I said, "he needed to get that out...if I didn't let him get that out of his system, he would just continue to be angry." His anger wasn't about me, it was really about many other things. Several weeks later that child in my class experienced the surprise and tragic death of his sister. I continued to stay in contact with the father, trying to give both him and his child things they needed. At the end of the year at our family gathering, the child's father came to me and told me how much I had meant to their families that year.

You build relationships. Sometimes they aren't calm sailing on flat seas. As with any relationship, there will be bumps in the road. We need to be mindful, for these are important people in our yearly and career-long Teacher's Journey. Parents are one of the key stakeholders in your growth and development. That may sound crazy to you, but having parents as strong allies will enable you to take more risks, try many new things that make your teaching better, and push the needle for growth and innovation within your school.

The Next Step

There is so much to take in during this chapter. From politics to parents the work of being an educator is not one thing, but many. While there may be a lot to reflect upon during this step in the journey, doing so will help you improve your practice and your ability to navigate the culture of your school.

Pre-Service Teachers

Understanding the school landscape can be a tricky business, and this chapter may have surprised and overwhelmed you. Let's take a look at this chapter's themes, one at a time.

1. Responsibility: Set up schedules for yourself and stick to them. If you have never been good at it, now is a great time to practice. While we can't simulate being fully responsible for kids in a classroom, you can learn to give yourself adequate time for the paperwork and other minutiae that can overrun your teaching life. Start learning to schedule in work times and personal times now!

2. Political Landscape: Anytime you walk into a school from now on, start to take notice of who has the power. Understanding the landscape may take a lot of time, but ask yourself questions. Is there a strong administration? Is there a group of teachers who have more privilege or do more? Are the parents active partners in what happens? Start recognizing these things now so that when you walk into your first school, you see them more clearly.

3. Ebbs and Flows: This one is simple. No matter how you are doing, reflection is one of the best ways to keep perspective. It will help you break down the rough times and get the most out of the best times. Start a journal, a blog, a collection of videos, anything that allows you to

reflect on your learning and your experiences. It will be a great way to improve and get the most out of your time.

4. Parents: When you are in your pre-service teaching, start making connections with parents. With the permission of your cooperating teachers, send home an introduction letter and try to send home a few positive notes each week so that by the end of the experience you have sent a positive note to every child and their parents.

New Teachers

1. Responsibility: You are most likely getting a crash course in responsibility with each day you walk into your classroom. Remember to look ahead. Add any paperwork that needs to be completed into your schedule now. Give yourself extra time. Also, make sure you have built your lesson plan template. Ask the administrator who checks your plans for feedback. It will be a great opportunity for you to get to know who they are and what they look for in the classroom.

2. Political Landscape: Take notice in the lunchroom, meetings, union meetings (if you have them), and in the side conversations people have in the hall.

Listen to everyone and start piecing together who holds what power? Remember in every school, even in the most engaging and caring communities, some stakeholders wield power.

3. Ebbs and Flows: If you haven't already, start keeping your reflections. Journals, blogs, videos, voice recordings, a website, sketchnotes... It doesn't matter what you use, just that you take time to reflect on where you are and where you are going.

4. Parents: Start by making at least five positive calls home every week. Even if you leave a message, just let parents know their child is doing something well. Do it for EVERY CHILD you have. Also, figure out how you want to communicate and interact with parents. Is it a newsletter? An app? Social Media? Phone? Find something that can work for you AND them.

Junior Teachers

1. Responsibility: At this point, you are fairly well-versed in the many responsibilities you have each day. Take a moment to reflect. Figure out what you do well. Now, what keeps you from doing well? Is that something you can get others to do or help you do? Is it something you can altogether eliminate? Or, is it something

you can make a conscious decision to improve upon? No matter the path forward, act on the thing that is keeping you from doing the things you do best. Be intentional about making that aspect of your teaching better.

2. Political Landscape: At this point, you should be able to identify in your school/district who has the power. Make yourself a list. What would you want your school to look like? What influence do you have with people who can help? How do you approach them? This is something you are more likely ready to do. Find your supporters and build from there.

3. Ebbs and Flows: Reflect, reflect, reflect. If you don't already keep a record of your reflections somewhere, it isn't too late. But, as you grow into the practice of reflecting, start to share those reflections with others. It will sharpen your reflection skills and help you become more intentional with how you look to improve.

4. Parents: Get parents involved. Yes, make the good calls home, write the positive notes, and over-communicate. But, now it is time to start doing more. Depending on what age and subject you teach, as well as the needs of your community, getting parents involved can take drastically

different appearances. Whether you invite them into your classroom, put on an event for them, create something to share with them, or any other idea, you build a strong bridge to the community by getting your parents involved in some way.

Master Teachers

1. Responsibility: Look to see who struggles with these responsibilities. Is there someone you can help? Who would benefit from your systems or style? Ask them if they would like to work on some task together. It will be a great way to begin developing a mentor relationship and opening the door for less experienced teachers to ask you important questions.

2. Political Landscape: Start working on using the influence you have to make positive changes. If you have hit this point in your career, you have undoubtedly developed some political capital within the school's structure. It is time to start using it to make positive changes in your school.

3. Ebbs and Flows: Start a group or encourage teachers to share their reflections with a small group of other teachers. This will be a first step toward collaborating and building trust that will

help those teachers be better at reflection and more likely to seek help on important topics.

4. Parents: Parents can make all the difference in the world. What do you want to change in the school? How can you leverage your positive relationship with parents to make a change?

Initiation

Chapter 6

Developing Our Spiritual Aides: Bringing New Teachers into The Profession

Year 1

A teacher's first year can be so many things. Mine was inspiring, chaotic, stressful, lonely, and taught me so much about who I was and who I wanted to be in the profession. This portion of your journey tends to be filled with many challenges. In retrospect, the challenges of my first year were minor compared to the work to shift an entire school culture, to change major programs, or to inspire a profession to think differently about its practices. Those are mountains. The problems I faced in my first year were mountains to me at the time. I just hadn't ever seen so much as a hill before then.

During that first year, I spent much of my teaching time in my classroom with my aide Deborah Lawton. Deborah had 16 years of experience as an aide in South Carolina, but was new to the school where I was working and to the area. I faced many of my problems in the classroom with her, but without other teachers in the district to help. My best help came from my parents who were former educators. Otherwise, there was so much I was afraid to show people.

My class included several students that needed

extra support. The balance of pride in what my kids were able to accomplish, and embarrassment at how poorly I handled certain situations was a hallmark of my first year. During that year, I helped kids learn to read, write, explore science, and work independently. I built relationships with families that still exist today. I also took my lumps in dealing with many obstacles and challenges. There were times when I felt my class was beyond my ability. There were times when I had absolutely no idea what to do, or where I was going. In fact, there were many times I was making things up as I went along. In the end, it was a mixed bag, filled with highs and lows, but somehow, whether because of me or in spite of me, my kids learned an incredible amount.

The first year is like that for so many teachers - if they are lucky. If not, it is mostly filled with doubt and struggle. One of the most frustrating things I reflect upon when thinking of my first year is that I couldn't actually be *great*. I could only just survive, hold on for the ride, or get by. My kids needed a great teacher, and they got me. I tried to be great - at times I may have even *been* great. But, there were no real supports to help ensure that I would be able to provide what my class needed.

My first-year experience was surprisingly typical for a teacher. The first major obstacle after finding a placement is learning to adapt to teaching in that first year. What amazes me is how many of the incredible teachers I have talked with felt the struggle of that year. Every one of us struggles at times, but almost none of us

118

avoid getting caught in the landslide of difficulties that comes with the first year of teaching.

Sylwia Denko felt the fear and anxiety of some of the remarkable pressures of being a teacher the night before her first day. "I thought to myself, oh my gosh, tomorrow 20 sets of parents will be sending their children off and trusting me with them, just me. Not only am I responsible for them, but I also have that huge responsibility to teach them reading, writing, math, science, social studies, spelling, but also how to be kind, how to respect one another, develop confidence, critical thinking skills, and creativity."

That is a pressure many teachers understand. Being responsible for helping a child grow into a good person is a monumental task. But, with that task comes incredible reward. Sylwia had an amazing first day and held a positive attitude toward her first year despite the challenges. "My first year was challenging, really challenging, but really wonderful. It is extremely difficult because you are experiencing changes that you've never experienced before, but at the same time you love it."

Sylwia credits so much growth to the value of learning and growing in that first year. "What was most difficult for me was that I am such a perfectionist. Having to learn all of the responsibilities that I had, on top of planning, sleeping, and everything else a teacher's role may be, makes it hard to figure out what is perfect, what is my best for my students."

Rae Hughart walked into her first day of teaching in a small town where she had never been before. "My first year teaching was incredibly challenging. I came with a very progressive mindset and philosophy on what I wanted my students to experience during the year, and I dealt with a lot of pushback." From having a strong student teaching experience, as Rae did, she was prepared to create great lessons and deliver them to kids. However, her first year "was an interesting lesson for me: teaching is more than just designing strong lessons, but to figure out how to work with the people around you, and the difficulties your kids are dealing with outside the classroom."

In her first year, she developed her "Teach Further" model which designed internship-style experiences for her students to engage in their learning. She built connections between learning and the community as well. It wasn't the pure teaching side that presented Rae with challenges, but taking that step beyond being a new teacher toward being a master teacher. Some of our teachers enter with excellent experiences and hit the ground running like Rae. Despite this, she realized that being an effective teacher meant more than just teaching.

"We were about 98% low income. I was a teacher from the moment I woke up 'til the moment I went to bed. I was after school with students, cooking dinner for students, breakfast, babysitting, and anything I could do to help my kids have a chance to learn." So many of us struggle with how to manage this type of commitment. Wanting the best for kids but also knowing that this pace is unsustainable over the course of a career is a huge challenge for all teachers, not just new ones.

Victor Small, Jr.'s experience was truly unique coming from his work as a recording artist. "My first day as a credentialed teacher was funny. I don't think that they knew that I rapped. I was trying really hard to hide that part of myself because I had gotten such rough response to showing that side of me. At any turn, if they get a whiff of hip-hop it would be a terrible idea. I dressed really clean cut, wore a suit, trying so hard to look good."

Fortunately for Victor, these first moments of his day would not be indicative of how he would teach, as who he is has been an important factor in connecting with kids. "It was the first day at a new school; I had 13 kids in my class. We opened the school. There was tons of time to prepare, but for some reason, I was so behind."

Despite having a shift from long-term subbing positions where he had 35 or 40 students, the responsibilities of the class being your own, and especially of opening a new school, were a challenge.

Stephanie Filardo's first-year experience is not uncommon. It was stressful, filled with learning, but also challenging to succeed. "I went from having no job on the first day of the school year, to having no classroom on my first day of having a job. I was co-teaching. I ran into struggles with seven different classrooms that I was working in."

Being stretched thin as a new special education teacher can be an incredible challenge, but one most teacher support staff experience. "It was really difficult to see the different classes and having one class where the teacher did not provide the structures the kids needed to learn. I came to find that I was placed to co-teach in a room to help classroom management." As you try to build relationships with the kids and the staff you support, having to learn as a new teacher to influence their teaching style and struggles with management is a terribly difficult way to begin.

Sarah Thomas remembers her first day as a blur. "I remember I was dressed in a pants suit and heels...my feet hurt a lot!" She does, however, more vividly remember her first year as one of her worst. "It was probably my worst year, or very close to my worst. I was still very young and immature for my age. I made a lot of rookie mistakes, and I wasn't in the most forgiving space to make those mistakes."

Teachers undoubtedly make mistakes, but in that first year, you are likely to make more mistakes than in any other. Not having the support to learn and grow makes it less likely that a teacher will succeed. Much of Sarah's work now with EduMatch is centered around connecting people and trying to make sure that we all have the support we need, no doubt inspired by some of the feelings of isolation she felt early on. "I wish back then I had a PLN. There was no Twitter, there was nobody outside of my school that I knew that I could ask questions or vent to that could understand exactly what I was experiencing." While she drew greatly from the support of her family, having good people outside of your family to lean on is an important part of being successful at just about anything.

Jon Corippo, not unlike many of us who came to the classroom later in life, had his first day in the classroom was as a permanent sub. He had to figure most of it out on his own, as he had nearly three months before he would have any formal teaching training. Unlike the other teachers whose journeys we have followed, Jon worked most of his early career on an emergency credential. While he worked through and managed to find successes early in his experience, it was during that time he also fell in love with teaching and knew he would make a career out of it.

Stacy Lovdahl found out that she would be teaching middle school science. "They called me the Sunday before the first day of school." She had no beginner teaching training and no education training. She was thrown right into the mix. After thirteen years as an environmental consultant, she was now teaching science. Her first year was an incredible challenge, but "thank goodness for the teachers who were in that building and helped me through that first year."

She also credited her amazing principal, James Ball, who sent her to classroom management training which helped her then and continues to help to this day. In December of her first year, she found out she needed to take the Praxis exam within six weeks in order to continue teaching. She passed the exam and got her license. Stacy found her life continuing with a work schedule that saw her up past midnight most nights, but she developed an idea that, "this may be my first year teaching eighth grade, but this is the only year they get to take eighth grade science."

While finding her style and learning to be the teacher she wished to be, "dry ice bubbling out of my pockets and creating explosions in the classroom," she relied on the teachers on her team to help her navigate her early years. Given the meaningful development and support she received early in her classroom career, Stacy's dedication to giving back to others and her aptitude for providing professional development for teachers all over North Carolina is a fitting outcome.

Kory Graham's career got off to a rocky start. She had difficulty finding a job right out of college, and spent the first months of the school year in Minnesota working at the Gap and walking everywhere she needed to go. Before finding her way into her own classroom, she worked as a substitute, volunteered, worked at a daycare, and finally worked as a part-time teacher. "It was very disappointing to me because I was not living my dream, not what I thought I was going to be doing. It was definitely some of the most character-building times of my life."

Finally, four years after graduation, Kory got a

full-time job teaching second grade. "The teacher I replaced was one of those amazing, all-star teachers, that got requested a lot." Just a week before school started Kory found herself working with two veteran teachers and two younger teachers, none of whom were on the same page. "I was always very confident in doing my own thing and going against the norm," which is something that has carried Kory throughout her career, but caused some difficulties in her first year.

While she was able to develop good relationships and have a positive experience with her colleagues, she found it easy to get caught in the middle of some of the drama that took place. Kory has become an educator who has worked to build connections and positive relationships, and these relationships have their roots early in her teaching journey.

As you face those first-year problems, whether as a teacher or a mentor, you must remember our goal is to ensure not only the success of students, but also that of the teacher. It can be so easy to succumb to negativity, yet none of our teacher heroes did. Remember that as a new teacher you almost certainly approached the journey with fire and excitement in hopes of making a difference for kids. As Jennifer Casa-Todd, an author, teacher librarian, and champion for student leadership has shared, "new teachers come in with a really keen sense of how they want it (school) to be better and different." However, unfortunately, we often allow negative forces in the school to beat that attitude out of them. "They acquiesce and do what has always been done."

We often allow the negative voices to be the loudest in the room. Why can't it be better? Why can't it be different from the way it's always been? That change starts with you. Whether you are simply experiencing these first-year problems for the first time, or you are a potential mentor, you have a role to play in whether or not things can be different.

Teaching is an incredible challenge. It is far too easy to succumb to negativity rather than persevere to make positive changes. The challenges you face and overcome can have a lasting impact on how you develop as an educator, the passions you find, and your ability to help both kids and teachers as your journey goes on. As you continue in your Teacher's Journey and aid others in their own, be mindful of your role. You can either allow negativity to spread, or you can shine with positivity.

At many points in my career, I have had the great fortune of working with enthusiastic and inspiring new teachers. In one particularly negative year, I remember banding together with a few other teachers in our small school to try and make a difference. We made it a point to turn around negative conversations in the teacher's lounge; we ate lunch in small groups together, went for walks with kids, and tried to push a positive message. It was good for us, the kids, and the school as well. It is a focus I found extremely important.

We spread positivity from a small group of teachers throughout the building. We refused to let negative narratives dominate the year, and it had a huge impact on our school's culture. How you choose to proceed is up to you, but if you remain complacent in the negativity, you allow it to spread throughout your school.

Junior Teaching

Despite my struggles and all the experiences that I brought with me to education, I still held in my heart a certain level of arrogance. I am referring more to the level of confidence that top athletes have rather than something braggadocious in nature. In my mind, I knew I was going to be great at teaching. I worked hard, tried to learn what I could, and continued to build connections with my families and students.

By the end of my third year, I was convinced I could easily be the best teacher in the school. Again, I was naive but passionate, and I desperately wanted to be great. By that time in my career, I was starting to get beyond survival mode and really assert myself as an educator.

I still look back at that year in amazement at the gains I made as a teacher. It was the year everything slowed down. I was ready to conquer anything and everything in teaching. In my mind, I was already a master teacher by the midpoint of that year. My lessons were incredibly engaging. I was creating most of the content myself, and my students were learning so much more than I could have dreamed. Everything went right for most of that year. There were few struggles and many triumphs. Part of it was luck; part the perfect chemistry that existed between myself and the kids I taught.

I was not surprised the following year in late fall when I was selected as the district's teacher of the year. With most things at the time, I played it down with comments like, "there's only 25 teachers in the whole school, I was bound to get it eventually." Deep down, however, I felt that I not only deserved this, but that I should apply for the county and state level teacher of the year awards as well. It was a lengthy application process, but of course, I should apply! The winners would be announced at the county teacher of the year luncheon in early spring.

When I walked into that luncheon, it could have been a scene out of a fairy tale. Lavish trim accentuated an opulent setting. I felt guilty for even being in a place like this, and despite my sports coat, I felt like nothing short of a tuxedo would have been appropriate.

It was a beautiful celebration, but also a defining moment in my career for several reasons. I had an opportunity to have a personal conversation with my superintendent. She was the person who had hired me, who had given me the opportunity to start my career. She was also the person who chose me to stay in the district repeatedly throughout the loss of positions and budget cuts. I can still hear her words, which remind me of how delicate a tightrope walk it was in my first years. She told me how she felt she was taking a chance on me, but that she expected me to be great. She also mentioned how over the first two years of my career, I gave her reason to question that choice many times, but she continued to trust and invest in my development. For a moment, I thought I had really arrived as a master teacher.

Then, as they began sharing the stories of the finalists for the county teacher of the year, that false sense of success came crashing down around me. As I heard one story after another of how these educators had an impact on more lives than just those in their classrooms, I realized I had so much more to learn. I had no idea how, but I knew I had to learn. Some of these teachers were making a global impact. It was another in a parade of humbling moments I have experienced as an educator. It was an awakening. There was so much more in the world of education than I had seen. It would be years before I developed an understanding of the larger world, and I am constantly learning new things about it.

The challenge comes for junior teachers in the transition from making an impact in your classroom, to making an impact on your school and beyond. As you experience success in the classroom, you will undoubtedly also have the requests and opportunities to branch out beyond just your classroom to share your knowledge, skills, and experiences with others. The shift from beginning teacher to the junior teaching phase which leads to master teaching is a big one. It is also a place where it seems so many teachers with promising beginnings become complacent, jaded, or disillusioned with improving within their profession.

It sounds simple, yet for younger educators, one of the most challenging things to learn during the journey is how to say no. You want to change the world. You want to be recognized for doing a great job. So, you take on all the new requests and responsibilities that everyone asks of you. Join this committee. Coach this sport. Lead this club. Pilot this program, take on new pre-service teachers, become an integral part of everything that happens within a school. Of course, doing all that can make your actual goal suffer. How can you really be effective and successful and making a difference in the lives of kids if you are doing ALL THE THINGS? You cannot. I can't either. You need to learn a few important things. The first is how to say no.

As Victor puts it, "you are not saying no, never, or no way" you are telling someone that you cannot accomplish that thing in the time they need. Instead of just saying, "no I can't," try saying something a little more. "I would love to help, but if you need this thing done by then, I won't be able to give it the attention it deserves."

Victor says, "Sometimes that's the conversation that has to happen."

In Victor's experience working at charter schools, there is incredible pressure for teachers to continue to say yes. The difficulty is that he and other teachers with whom he worked were always, "willing to fill in and do what's necessary." This can create a difficult and dynamic situation where "people are willing (to help), but also not willing to say no. They are always willing to give up their time." There isn't anything wrong with giving up your time for the betterment of your school or students. What happens, however, is that we often give up too much of our time to the detriment of our students and ourselves.

Might we successfully do more? My first response matches Victor's: learn to say no. But in doing so, also learn to identify what you are most passionate about or strongest at doing. So often we focus on what we are bad at and try to get better. Instead, it can help to focus on what we are good at, and then learn to say yes to things that utilize those skills. If you are excellent at classroom management, work in that capacity as a leader in the school. You do not need to be the leader of all the things; instead, a school should have many leaders in a variety of different areas. Ideally, you understand what you care about and what skills you have that can impact that area.

As a junior teacher, you should have a firm grasp of what you've developed as well as areas where you are less strong. Choose to be a leader in the areas of your strengths and passions. Let someone else take care of the rest.

I have worked in an extremely small school. At times, especially during the junior teacher phase of my journey, I said yes to far too many things. It didn't matter if it was something I was passionate about or that I knew about. What mattered was that I could be a part of it. What mattered was starting to grow into a deeper leadership role within my school.

I felt it was something I had to do, so I did *all the things*. My teaching suffered at times. It wasn't bad, but it also wasn't to my own lofty standards. I understand the desire to be a part of things and to ensure that opportunities exist for kids. What I didn't understand at the time was that by doing all the things I had taken on, I was missing so much around me. I wasn't doing any of the things exceptionally, nor was I teaching at my best on most days. So, what else can we do to ensure things get done?

Sarah Thomas had an experience like my own. She found herself being quickly and frequently called upon to do more as she established herself as a teacher: so many requests and so little time. In addition to learning to say no, she learned to delegate activities. Not only did she learn to allow others to do work that suited them, but she also started creating student-led teams to accomplish tasks that were falling on her shoulders.

But, Sarah knew she was going to survive and really move toward successful teaching when she found her perfect fit in a new school working with technology. Sarah knew she would be able to thrive as an educator when she woke up excited about her work. "I always loved going in and being with the kids. That part never changed, but now I was excited about the people I worked with, and the things I was doing."

Finding that passion for what you do is

important. Like many other educators, Sarah always had a passion for working with kids, but the reality is, that passion can only carry you so far. You need to be able to find ways to get excited about the other parts of your work at times, to be excited about the challenges, the content, or your coworkers. In retrospect, I also found that excitement in my third year. I finally knew enough about my coworkers, about my school, and about what I was doing that I could find excitement in everything I did.

Kory Graham spent nearly four years trying to achieve her dream of becoming an educator. She worked through various challenges in her first year and learned to succeed. "In the early years, it never occurred to me I wouldn't survive teaching; teaching was who I was." In year 12 of her career - her first year teaching kindergarten - she had her first doubts.

It was her return to the classroom for the first time in over two years. The first two years back was her most challenging. Kory felt frustrated, and she struggled with her move to the new school. "Between those two years, I felt like I could not be a teacher at this school. I was physically exhausted, mentally exhausted, and emotionally exhausted."

Kory found her most stressful and significant challenges in the school that was in a lower socioeconomic area. "Working in a school where kids are economically more well off, it is generally easier." She found the work rewarding, but also more taxing on her.

Beyond those two years, Kory continued to grow and learned to become an inspiring kindergarten teacher. She took those years as a chance to reflect. "I had a lot of people looking out for me in those two years, and in some ways, that's comforting. If there is a teacher that is having a challenging year, remind them that this year will pass. When you have those tough classes, you really refine your teaching skills. Even though (a challenging year) provides a lot of headaches and stress, it makes us better in the end." This message illustrates how Kory continues to share and grow with people all around her. She is dedicated to empowering others and lifting them up.

While some of us face doubts and struggles, others always knew survival was in their future. Stephanie Filardo never doubted that she would survive teaching. "It's really a matter of surviving the circumstances teaching puts us in, but I never really thought about it as something I needed to survive." Her difficult first year could have ended her career, but she was determined to succeed.

Part of that success was moving away from a politically toxic environment. Finding a new position was a large part of what helped launch her career forward. Landing in a new school where the atmosphere was more supportive provided Stephanie with an opportunity to move beyond survival mode and start to thrive as an educator.

We all encounter this hurdle. If you are successful as a teacher in your beginning years, you will find yourself with new responsibilities and opportunities. How you learn to manage your time and resources will change your path going forward. While you may find this exciting or frustrating, you should (as always) not face these challenges alone. You are not the only teacher to experience these challenges, so don't plan on trying to overcome them alone.

Some educators find incredible success early on in their career. Rae Hughart started moving past the survival stage earlier in her career than most educators. "I think I realized I was going to survive teaching when I started to develop the 'Teach Further' model" late in her first year and continuing throughout her career, "as I got into designing unit-based internships for kids." Rae found her purpose in having students who were, "becoming passionate about what they were doing," which made her realize she was going to really be a teacher.

There is something special about learning to make teaching your own and not just following along with what someone else is doing. You move from floating down the rapids on a raft, to holding the paddle. You are no longer solely at the mercy of outside forces; you are finally in control. As with many of us who reflect on how we reached this empowered feeling in our teaching, Rae credits her mentors.

Like Rae, Sylwia Denko thrived early in her teaching career. While her first year was difficult, she also was able to jump into the profession with the passion and experience most teachers don't possess at the start of their career. Despite her early successes, of course she was faced with difficult times, as any developing educator will experience over the course of their journey.

Sylwia left an observation early in her career feeling deflated. "It was one of those unannounced observations where everything that could have gone wrong, went wrong." Most of us have had a day where our best-laid plans fell apart right in front of us. She was incredibly upset to think she had left a poor impression on her administrator. She walked into the meeting feeling awful.

An important moment followed as her administrator said, "I don't think you realize how good you are." That moment was uplifting and empowering for her. It gave her the confidence to invite her administrator into her classroom again in the future and shaped her perspective that a good teacher, "can take a negative situation and turn it into a positive opportunity for kids."

The adolescent phase of your Teacher's Journey will allow you many opportunities to improve and transcend the times where you are struggling to make a larger impact on the lives of kids. At some point, if you answered a call to education, you had hopes of making a difference in the world. This period is the crucial time in your career where you can either find your wings and take off into years of excellence, or where you can be dragged down and destroyed by the difficulties of extra responsibilities and expectations.

During this part of your journey, you will find the opportunity to influence your students and your school in new and exciting ways. People will begin to trust you with important duties in your school, and you will have a hard time saying no. Being successful during your Junior Teacher years requires lots of things, but three things that we see in our teacher heroes can help you maintain the success you've found.

First, figure out what matters to you in your school. It is important to find some things you are passionate about in the profession.

Next, only do the extra things that you love. If you don't love them, they will just be a drain on you and your ability to teach well.

Finally, learn how to pick your battles. You can't always win, and sometimes when you win, you will lose. Learn what is worth fighting for and how to address those battles. That means figuring out what you are willing to lose in order to fight the battle. It means learning who you need to address and what they care about to most successfully achieve your aims.

Master Teachers

At no point will I consider myself to have mastered teaching. If I ever do feel that way, I should probably stop doing it. So, while there may be other definitions, I will stick with what I previously defined: a master teacher is someone who has the ability to regularly plan and implement educational experiences that empower kids to learn. At the same time, s/he also has a positive impact on their school, local, and professional communities.

Many times, I have thought I was a master teacher, but I didn't know what it meant. In one sense a master teacher is simply one who wants to improve upon the impact one has in the world. I started this part of my journey when I gained a greater understanding of what my impact could be. Being a master teacher isn't about being perfect, or knowing everything. Simply put, a master teacher makes a positive difference in the lives of their students, colleagues, and education community.

While many times in my teaching career I experienced challenges that led me toward becoming a "master" teacher, there are none that focused me in my purpose of connecting teachers and kids like the time when I lost my class.

Over the year that I had known my new CSA, he had only really seen me trying desperately to sift through the mountains of incredible ideas that come with being a newly connected educator. At times the year was filled with incredible teaching moments, but at times it was frantic and chaotic because I still believed I was the greatest thing in education (or at least I wanted to be) and that meant doing ALL THE THINGS! I had to do all the incredible things I was seeing everyone share on social media. Of course, I did; my kids deserved it!

What people often fail to mention when sharing these incredible experiences is the number of times they fail. So, I failed often. My CSA hadn't been in my room for many of the great successes, but he sure did witness a lot of the disasters. Explaining to him why a student was at the nurse after another student was testing his UFO design during Genius Hour was a prime example of what my classroom was to him in our first year together.

After a few months of seeing my alternative learning space filled with stability balls, cots, homemade stools, camping chairs, yoga mats, and other alternative seating options for kids to learn comfortably, he had had enough. As always, my classroom was in creative disarray. I was bad at managing paper and hadn't learned a better way yet. I was also learning along with the students on how to build and work in this new environment successfully.

Rarely during my career as a classroom teacher was I ever accused of having a "clean room." Kids make messes, and I focused on learning. There were times when we ran out of time to clean the mess because we weren't done *doing*. Those times, I would hastily clean things in the morning and set my classroom back to square one. When projects were going to take multiple days, I left them. This meant that there was almost always a part of the room that was messy. Learning tends to look like that anyway, so I never worried.

That is, I never worried, until I was written up for having a disorganized classroom.

I had a talk with the CSA, but I never had any help or instruction on making the space better. What I needed, and had asked for, was an opportunity to come in and work, maybe even get half a day to finish the original plan I had started in the summer (we only had two days to create the rooms because of construction, and I was teaching in an incomplete masterpiece).

On a Monday morning in December, a month that included many projects, I arrived over an hour before school, as was my routine. I was asked to see the CSA before the day began. At that point that I was told, "your classroom is not a learning environment."

The directive was for me to make plans for that Friday for a substitute to teach my class in the library. We had done class in the library several times already that winter, courtesy of struggling heating systems and temperatures below 55 degrees Fahrenheit in our room on some days. During that Friday I would have another teacher come in and redesign my classroom. I could work with her on making it "what it was supposed to be," so that I could be successful for the remainder of the year.

Welcome to the lowest point in my teaching

career.

I was coming off being the district teacher of the year, flying through my Masters in School Administration, and just starting to figure out how to apply some of the coolest things I was learning from the hundreds of teachers I had connected within the past year. Then I had my bubble burst.

The stability balls were deflated; the room was decorated with chevrons and eerie stick figures from Teachers Pay Teachers. There isn't anything wrong with that being your room (except those stick figures...they are scary), but it wasn't *mine*. Imagine designing the perfect living space only to be removed from that space and asked to live in a hotel for a year; not because there was something structurally wrong with the space, but because it didn't fit what other people expected.

That was my teaching life for the rest of the year. I was teaching in a hotel room. While the room was slightly more organized, the systems weren't mine. They were someone else's.

I was incredibly sad going to work each day. Walking into someone else's space, using someone else's systems of organization, and trying to face my students and the staff was embarrassing. It drained my motivation in ways I had never experienced as a teacher.

There were many times in my career when I almost didn't make it as an educator, but this was the only time when I thought that leaving teaching might be something that I wanted.

How did I survive? Part of me was ready to leave

the district and seek employment elsewhere immediately, even if that meant leaving teaching. Part of me knew I had to find a way forward.

What lit my path during those darkest times? The light of my many mentors. When I had no idea what to do, they were there. I spoke to many different people about how I felt, what I was experiencing, and how to improve my situation in the long term. This wasn't a problem I could learn my way out of through acquiring new skills or receiving coaching. I needed the experience of the good people I had been collecting in my life. Their support, their ability to help me see the issues from many perspectives, and my trust in them helped me stabilize my career. It would have been easy to abandon the journey and accept defeat, but instead, I overcame.

This was one of the greatest trials of my teaching journey. I learned more about what was expected of me from my new CSA. I also learned how I could apply those expectations to my own teaching style and ability.

During the next 18 months, I changed dramatically. I went from being someone the CSA viewed as a liability to someone he trusted with school planning. While I didn't agree with him on many issues, he knew that I was someone who learned about everything I could, would reach out beyond the school for advice, and was willing to change and improve.

During that time, I also doubled down on my resolve to help teachers avoid those feelings of loneliness and isolation. My ability to develop positive relationships with mentors and coaches had both saved and inspired my career on many occasions. I knew that not everyone would have the same way of absorbing content and learning as I did, but I also recognized the abundance and value of communities in education that are available to teachers if they are willing to connect to people. This is why, despite the number of educators on Twitter, it is not necessarily the best way to learn for everyone.

Some people prefer other social networks, like Pinterest, Google Plus, Voxer, or Facebook groups. Others need you to help them directly by connecting them to the specific people and knowledge they need. Realizing that we all need to learn and grow but - that not everyone learns in the same way, I came to an important reflection. How can I be a conduit that helps connect people in the world?

Over the course of time, my aim of being a knowledge conduit for others morphed beyond just teachers. I also wanted to allow students to experience the world in a new way.

The isolation my students felt was very real. Many of them had little experience of the world and no idea what the world's opportunities could be. So, we built a bridge to connect our classroom to as many places as possible. That bridge allowed me as an educator to find many opportunities that spurred me forward. In turn, I created the Global Audience Project as a place for teachers and students to find classes around the world to share experiences with one another. From that incredibly low point in my career that involved many failures, I struggled and built many more successes.

Having overcome a "great ordeal" in my Teacher's Journey, I began focusing sincerely on reaching out to others, on translating the experiences I had to help them (Campbell, 1993). The defining moments on my Teacher's Journey lay in the resolve I developed over those few months of "hotel teaching." I could have accepted the defeat and moved on, but instead, I worked to grow and improve. That growth pushed the needle in some classrooms to develop more alternative seating and design options, as well as some different approaches to teaching Math, Science, and Social Studies in the primary classrooms.

When I look back on that episode now, I am grateful; not because I felt like I needed to tear apart my classroom that day, but because I became determined to find my way forward. Taking full advantage of the network of dozens of potential mentors I had found allowed me to move into a stage in my teaching career where I understand more about how I can apply what I learn, and how to make changes successfully on both small and large scales. I think of those things as the hallmarks of master teachers.

When I spoke to each of our Teacher Heroes, I did so with the understanding that there was something special about them. Each of them is a master teacher in my eyes. While some of them may have not yet extended their careers long enough to have many believe they are in that category, I can see it in what they do and say. None of them claims to have "mastered" teaching, but they understand who they are as educators. They do what they can to make teaching better in their immediate space and beyond, which is what makes them masters.

One of the most common themes amongst our teacher heroes is their reluctance to call themselves master teachers. Each of them knows there are significant challenges they must continue to overcome, and each understands that there is much more they have to learn. The remarkable consistency with which these teachers deflect the term "master" from themselves is a testament to their quality as educators, that they seek to continually improve and thus find the label in opposition to their nature. Through struggles and continued growth, master teachers learn to inspire others while improving themselves. Our *Teacher Heroes* are no different.

"In terms of considering myself a master teacher? I would say no, but it's hard to define," Dr. Sarah Thomas shares. She refers instead to being a seasoned teacher. Through the various struggles and perseverance in her career, Sarah has come to value relationships and authenticity. Those two things have not only helped her in the classroom, but in the continuation of her career outside a school building as well. "I still do learn and grow; learning to be the best for our kids is something we should all aspire to do."

Sarah has lived this statement through her work building connections between good people. "Everyone who teaches me something is a mentor in some way, shape, or form; some kids have been my mentors in various ways as well." Sarah embodies what it means to be a master teacher in that she finds ways to learn, grow, and support others in the pursuit of improving education for kids and teachers.

Rae Hughart realized she had much to learn, and the understanding that she does not know everything, which is an important aspect of being a great educator. "I would be thrilled to be called a master teacher, but I am not sure what that means. For me, I envision an expert, but I have so much more to learn, especially from my kids." Rae is able to see her need to continue learning.

Like many of us, Rae has overcome difficulties in her teaching career that have helped her move toward being a master teacher. After moving to a new town and starting a new career, she struggled at times. Through connecting with others, she was able to begin learning. "A low point in my career was working with my first set of students. I really wasn't sure how to help the students. They didn't understand why they had to be at school. They had real issues, issues that I had never dealt with and figuring out how to make education purposeful for them was a low point: realizing I didn't know how to address those concerns."

She realized that building relationships with those students and bringing value to the content for her kids were all part of how she would be an effective teacher. Bringing herself out of that low point with the help of others is the embodiment of the understanding that we hope to have in master teachers. When teaching gets difficult, and it will, learning how to build and value relationships will help get you through.

One of the great things that makes Rae a master teacher is her ability to identify and connect with people who can help her learn. "I have had the ability to present at a number schools and conferences on the Teach Further Model, and the amount of learning I take from the people in the room, especially working with them after the presentation on a more personal level, has been magic." Learning to learn continuously and from anyone is an important piece of being a master teacher.

Kory Graham emphatically denies being a master teacher. "NO! I do not consider myself a master teacher. I am a good teacher." Kory would never admit to being great; it isn't part of her personality. She even has a difficult time accepting the praise of others. "I am always amazed when I share ideas, and people think the things I do are amazing. I just don't see that."

Of course, Kory has shared ideas that connected her kids to classrooms around the world, built elementary coding stations for her classes and found ways to build significant instructional innovation into the classroom. But despite her innovations, Kory will contend that she is "just a teacher." Part of this is her personality, but also part of it is that she feels like she can always be better.

What really makes Kory an amazing master teacher is her ability to find ways to connect people, learning, and reflections, and transform them into remarkable experiences for kids and teachers. Kory knows herself and how she learns: "I am always asking questions and have an intrinsic motivation to always be getting better. I don't need a certificate for that or to be an ambassador for anything, that's not what makes me run."

Knowing who you are as a learner is an important part of being able to learn and grow on your own. The ability to take control of your own learning and then use your new learning to impact other people's learning is something every master teacher ought to be able to do.

Sylwia Denko is another one of many educators who decline the title of Master Teacher. "I never want to get to the point in my career where I feel like I have mastered it." Sylwia's viewpoint is wise beyond her four years in the classroom. While she holds reservations about the idea that anyone could master a thing as complex as teaching after such a short time, it is her understanding of how to continue growing that helps me view her as a master teacher. "Year after year whether you have been teaching for three years or forty years, you are going to come across experiences you've never had before, and you continue learning and growing."

Not only does Sylwia recognize that there is no full mastery, but she has learned to transition into improving the practices in both her classroom and in the classrooms of others. "I worked really hard my first year to lay the groundwork for my lessons and with my craft. In the beginning, I was spending a lot of time on things I didn't have to, but as I have grown, I have found ways to be more efficient with my time, which allows me to do more and different things."

Sylwia has managed to maintain an excellent classroom, while branching out to offer learning opportunities in her district, outside of her district, and with upcoming pre-service teachers. Her dedication to continuing to learn, becoming more efficient with her time, and learning to empower others is an important characteristic of any master teacher.

Stephanie Filardo is another educator who, while admitting that some might see her as a master teacher, feels that there is so much for her to learn and do in her career. "I come from this place where I know there is a lot that I have to learn still and a lot of ways that I still need to grow." The ability to blend her experiences, struggles, and learning is part of what makes Stephanie an excellent educator.

One experience that pushed her confidence and has prompted people she works with to see her as a master teacher happened at a conference with her school district. She was in another session when she saw a tweet asking for the presenter of a session on using Google Classroom to show up. She told her principal what was happening and left the session she was in to offer help. She stepped in on the spot to teach the group about Classroom, and show them how using Classroom had transformed her own work with students. This was an impromptu moment to share with others what she knew, how it impacted real kids in her classes, and give them a WHY behind using a digital tool with kids.

While she was presenting, many of her fellow staff members and their principal made their way to the session because it was going so well. "The fact that I was able to talk about that competently and confidently was a huge deal." It gave her the feeling of confidence that master teachers generally have when sharing their learning. The ability to tell others both *what* and *why*, while using examples from your work is a hallmark of master teaching.

Victor Small, Jr. has acknowledged, "I don't see myself as a master teacher, but I can see why some people might say that." He can be honest in his self-reflection of being great at some aspects of his work, while still needing to learn more. "I realized people saw me as a master of classroom management when the way in which administrators spoke about me with students changed. They would say, 'everyone gets along with Mr. Small...what did you do to him?' whenever one of my students came to them."

Victor didn't always excel at classroom management and relationships with his kids. He had to struggle, learn, and grow. He wrestled with the expectations of his school in comparison to what was practical in his classroom. "I thought, if I could come up with exceptions, it shouldn't be zero tolerance. But I was part of enforcing that. It was a struggle because it put me in difficult situations with students." Victor brings his positivity and passion to his work.

He also pushed his kids to ask questions and to model his expectations for students in his classroom management practices. "When you teach like that, you teach to think and ask questions, but you don't ask questions (yourself), it is counterintuitive to what you are trying to do. Once I did that, I felt like things got a lot better for me."

Since then, Victor has continued to learn and improve upon his methods, including his work with restorative justice. Being excellent at something isn't a reason to stop learning or improving, it is just a reason to start sharing what you know about it. Sharing his knowledge of restorative justice is something Victor has been doing with regularity in recent years.

Like the rest of our master teachers, Victor tries to find and learn from as many intelligent people in the room. "You'll never truly know everything because you don't know what everyone knows in their own head, that's why we talk to them."

So, now that you are a master teacher, we have come to the end of our Teacher's Journey, right? Not by a long shot. Teaching, like the Hero's Journey, doesn't end with conquering the objective. Part of being a master teacher, and in fact part of our Teacher's Journey, is to find our way home. In doing so, we return home changed. Home doesn't mean a place in this journey, but an ideal. We come back to our classrooms, schools, and most importantly to our profession, with a different idea of what we can bring to this world.

Creating a better future for teachers and education demands that we develop master teachers. Becoming a master teacher is an incredibly challenging step in the journey, and in fact, it is where our path is hopefully leading. Making this leap helps us as educators learn to productively give to our school community and to the greater education community.

An important piece of this development is becoming a critical learner. It is not good enough just to learn everything, but instead to learn what you need. It is also important to learn how to work with others to figure out what they need. Being a master teacher means learning to find ways to influence your community and beyond through your teaching and expression.

Our job, once we achieve some level of understanding (which I refer to as master teaching), is to build upon that understanding for the betterment of the profession. Teaching can become transformational in practice for both students and educators if those of us who have found some level of mastery return to the practice and begin the process again. We work within our own journeys, but also to enhance the journeys of others as mentors or coaches.

The Next Step

This chapter laid out the stages of our journey through the eyes of many different educators. The reflections and challenges we will explore now will help you make a transition into your next stage, or excel where you are now.

Pre-Service Teachers

It is worth noting that the parallel that can exist between your journey as a pre-service teacher from its beginning until now and the journey of a new teacher working your way toward mastery. Take this time to reflect on where you were as you entered your pre-service teaching education. Spend a few minutes with each of the following questions:

1. How have you changed? What have you learned? What are you excited about?
2. What can you pass on to those who will come after you?
3. Stepping in well prepared as a new teacher involves experience, reflection, and keeping your good people. How are you developing those characteristics right now?

New Teachers

You are neck deep in it now, but with every new experience, you can learn and improve. While your new world may be moving at light speed, it does slow down.

1. As this book reiterates many times, find good people and don't be afraid to use their experiences and knowledge to help

you grow.

2. Reflect on everything. All you create, all you attempt, should come with deliberate and purposeful reflection. What went well? What didn't? How could it be better?

3. What did you learn from the many new teacher stories? How do you move to the next step of the journey?

Junior Teachers

Welcome to an amazing point in your career. This point in your career will be your fertile ground to grow. Your early experiences in the classroom have sown seeds that will become your passions in your career. Or, it could all become a set of shackles. How you proceed from here will impact your experience for the rest of your time in the profession. How do we ensure you grow in your passions and become the master teachers our kids and our profession need?

1. Our successful Junior Teachers have become reflective practitioners. They are discovering their passions in education and the world. What is important to you in your classroom? In your school? In education in general?

2. Start focusing on what is important to you. Learn to say no to things that take away from your passions, profession, and personal well-being. Find people who are

154

successfully doing what you love and start building relationships.

Master Teachers

Now that you have "arrived," you are in the amazing position to make real changes on a significant level. A large part of fostering change is cultivating the growth of others who believe in your changes. Here are some ways to start:

1. Be available. You can't force other teachers to trust you or to respect you. But you can build quality relationships with others and start to share your understandings with others. All that starts by being available for Junior and New Teachers when they are looking for support.

2. What can you give back? You aren't the only person who has something to contribute, nor are you the TOP expert at most things, but the way you share the message may resonate with people. How can you share your passions with others? Take the opportunities to share with others the things you love.

Chapter 7

How We Grow Teachers through Personal and Professional Development

When I was a boy, my dad coached EVERYTHING. He coached all the sports we played: soccer, baseball, and basketball. He also coached football, which none of us played. He donated time and resources to our local recreation center.

I asked him one time, "why do you do so much?"

He responded simply, "this our community...it is my job to give back to it."

Later my dad explained to me that when he was a boy, people often would donate their time, money, or resources to help the young people in the community. It was his cultural norm, going beyond taking care of himself to take care of others. Even though he grew up in a different community, giving back meant he would give back to the place he lived. I grew up with this example, and so for me, giving back to the community seems like something everyone ought to do.

We exist in three main communities as educators. The first is your local community where you live. Many people give something to their home. Giving to your local community is personal and often also depends on your community's needs.

Next is your school community. Whether you work and live in the same town or not, educators often give back to the places where they work. Educators frequently organize events, develop support systems, or donate time and resources to the young people in their school community. For as long as I have worked in a school, I have seen and felt this sense of "giving back" in many ways.

The third area, the one which seems most underrepresented, is our professional community. Many educators feel like they might not have anything to give. Others may respond with, "What's in it for me?" or "I don't have time for that." The truth is, all of us have had help at one point or another.

Everyone starts out treading water, thrashing for the life-preserver. No matter your path into education, you have had at some point at least minimal coaching, and at best, a high-quality mentor relationship. The education profession increases its demands every year, and each year, new and developing teachers are expected to meet the ever-changing needs of diverse populations. Yet, as our profession is most in need of our contributions, I see fewer and fewer teachers giving back professionally. Our community of professional educators is in need. How are you giving back?

Effective Use of Coaching and Mentoring

Mentors are essential to the Teacher's Journey. They are in many ways among the most crucial components to success. Yet, as teachers, we struggle to identify mentors throughout our careers. Often, we also struggle to transition into mentorship roles for others in our profession.

Having spent the past several years listening to
educators discuss their ideas on teacher development, I
have concluded: **one of the most severe deficiencies
in our professional community is the lack of
genuinely developed mentor/mentee relationships.**

At the beginning of this book and throughout the
first six chapters, we have explored stories of my own
and others struggles. On each of the early steps in my
journey, I found myself increasingly secluded. I worked
on an island with very few people to call upon for help.
Even with some people whom I respected and trusted, I
felt like I was the only one. I know now that I am not.

It took a long time for me to find and connect
with people who would mentor me in my educational
development. It was a process I learned, in many
respects, on my own. In my early career, there were
several people with whom I enjoyed working. This
allowed me to survive, but despite getting better as a
teacher, I never really grew into my potential during
that time.

One of the greatest obstacles we have to
continued growth and learning, as well as making a
difference in the classroom, is the absence of someone
to guide us through the changes. I can learn almost
anything on my own (except masonry... I learned that
even with YouTube I can't lay a subfloor). Do you want
to put new skills into practice or make changes in your
classroom? Making fundamental shifts in practices will

come with new challenges and experiences. Having someone who has recently been through something similar will help you understand what to expect. It also gives you someone to confide in, who you can trust and can guide you toward growth. Yet, most teachers don't think of themselves either as a mentor or in need of a mentor.

Along every Hero's Journey, a hero will receive crucial guidance and support from mentors. The Teacher's Journey should be no different, but in many cases, our experiences fall short.

Think for a moment. When I ask you, "Who was your mentor?" what is your first reaction? My guess is that you, like the vast majority of educators, were arbitrarily assigned a mentor based on your teaching assignment. You, like many other teachers, were randomly assigned another teacher (whom you may have even had to pay) to be your most trusted advisor and advocate. You may have had a great relationship with this person. Maybe it was a perfect match. That is, however, not always the case. Developing relationships and trust isn't an easy thing to do. It takes time, experience, and an understanding that you share common goals or paths.

I don't want to discount these people. They were assigned to you for a reason. But, let me be clear: mentors don't use checklists to know if their job is done. If you and this person used a checklist, chances are the relationship something other than mentorship. Let's pretend for a moment that you were fortunate to find the perfect match and had a great, healthy, and valuable mentor relationship as a new teacher. Did you continue to grow with that person? A healthy mentor relationship continues to develop until the difference in experience has disappeared. One of the beautiful things about great mentor relationships is that while the mentoring may end, the relationship never really dissipates.

Now, allow me to rephrase the question: "Who are your mentors?"

By this I am not referring to some person whom you shared a year with early in your career, checking off boxes, but a person who helps guide your experiences now. If you don't have an answer, don't worry, you soon will.

A common misconception among teachers along their journeys is that you only need a mentor at the beginning of your career. Even some of the greatest teachers I know have referred to getting a mentor mid-career as "silly" or "unnecessary because I have been teaching 20 years." Yet mentorship is not a one-time deal. As we face new trials and undertake new steps of our journey, we need additional guidance. Learning from the experiences of others should not be considered only for new teachers.

So often we fail in education to understand what mentors do, what roles they fill, and how they differ from the roles of coaches and administrators. I failed in understanding this for years. While these titles can at times overlap, they perform very different roles in our lives and in our development as educators. It is crucial that educators understand what mentors provide us, to find success and balance in our lives.

Education is a personal profession. We learn things and share them as we develop along our own paths. We create personal connections with our students and their families as well as our co-workers. Yet for more than four years of my career, some of the most important developmental years for an educator, one thought had never occurred to me: I am not alone. I have spent most of my life being slightly different (ok, sometimes very different) and for the longest time, I felt alone. Have you ever felt alone in the classroom? Whether yes or no, think about why.

I felt alone in my first year for so much of the time. My closest friends and mentors weren't classroom teachers. While they were, in large part, the saving grace for my early career, I still had to fall back on the echoes of former teachers with whom I had lost touch. For much of my first two years, I survived. I pretended, I stole, I begged, I borrowed, I failed, and I persevered. Notice what is missing? I was living and teaching in survival mode.

In year three, for the first time, I started to fly, to thrive with my teaching. I was finally the gift to the world of teaching I anticipated being in my first days. Only, I wasn't really.

I was having success, but I didn't understand how to scale that success. I surely didn't understand how to build upon it or what it would mean to continue growing.

Having sat in the room with so many other great

teachers during the ceremony for our county teachers
of the year, I never felt so out of place or inadequate. I
had had some great experiences in teaching up until
then, but I didn't really feel worthy of sitting in that
room. To that point I never had felt like a drop of water
in the bucket; I was always a big fish in a small pond.
Yet, learning about how real master teachers were
making a huge difference in their classrooms, schools,
and in education as a whole, I realized I was still so far
from being a great teacher. I had in some ways
plateaued and needed this shock to inspire me to be
more.

In saying all this, I simply acknowledge that I
found a level of teaching and learning over the years,
mostly through determination, will, and fortune. I could
have just as easily succumbed to the crucible of
teaching, or missed the fortuitous circumstances.

What could have made my experience better?
How can we learn from the mistakes made along our
journeys to improve the path for future educators? One
common theme that teachers have expressed is having
someone else with whom to share your experiences.
Being a teacher can be lonely enough; doing it without
another teacher in a similar stage of their journey with
whom to share your ups and downs can be even more
difficult.

Still, a large part can be improved by
understanding the roles of coaching and mentoring.
From there, we can begin to understand how we find
and develop our own mentors, and to build the culture

of growth within the profession.

Coaching

Most teachers receive a "mentor" when they begin their first full year of teaching. The experiences developed with these mentors are varied at best. The concept of the first-year mentor in education was created with good intentions; new teachers shouldn't be alone. New teachers need allies, friends, confidants, and in general, people to help them find their way through an incredibly demanding experience. Many school districts take that responsibility seriously, and so attempt to place a master teacher with a new one.

It is impossible, however, to fully understand the intricacies required to develop a strong mentor relationship. Those relationships are built on trust, respect, and an understanding that this person has experiences from which you can learn. The relationship most first-year teachers create with their assigned mentors is not typically a mentoring relationship, but rather one of coaching.

Hearing the stories of so many educators, it is increasingly apparent that we don't understand the difference between coaches and mentors. We also have difficulty identifying either. Most "mentors" that are assigned do little to serve the role of mentor. They do, however, usually play an important role in our development. Instead, most of our assigned mentors are expected to give us certain skills, much like a coach.

Sometimes the mentor relationship develops.
Mentoring is not now, nor will it ever be, about learning
to master a task. We need to master tasks, but to seek
true mentorship from our coaches, or to assume our
mentors are merely there to transmit skills, is a striking
misconception that plagues the teaching profession.

Coaches, or helpers, play an important role in the
Hero's Journey. Typically, heroes need new skills to be
successful on their journey. They must learn these skills
to overcome the trials. Such skills are apart from the
experience they gain from mentors, but regardless are
indispensable to success.

As a teacher hero, you need new skills as well.
Learning these skills will allow you to find success on
your journey, and good coaches will make this much
easier. There is, however, more to becoming a great
teacher than just skills development.

Still, coaching is extremely valuable to getting
better at anything. A coach can identify needs and help
assess what you need to improve. There are many
important distinctions between coaching and
mentoring. Understanding those distinctions can make
your journey more manageable and lead to greater
success.

The Difference Between Coaching and Mentoring

The first-year coaching relationship is extremely
valuable if established correctly. New teachers need a
guide through the murky waters of a new school. There
are often a number of simple procedural matters, "how

tos," and relationships that can be shared by a first-year coach. So, when you think, "I don't need a mentor anymore...I have been doing this for a while," you are really thinking of that coach who helped you acclimate to your new school. During the first year, calling a *coach* a mentor leads to a confusion of the relationship. While some coaches eventually become mentors, the roles are inherently different. New teachers need time to develop relationships and understand their own needs so they can identify mentors throughout their career.

Coaching and mentoring are different, but necessary parts of professional development. While they are important, the difference is equally important if we are going to understand how to do either well. Coaching is about teaching a skill. Need to create more effective lesson plans? Want to learn to incorporate technology into your curriculum? Need to hit a curveball? You need a coach. A coach doesn't need to be someone you trust intimately. Instead, you must simply believe they know what they are doing, and that they want what is best for kids. You don't even need to like them (though it does help). What you need is an understanding that they know this skill and can help you learn it. Their job is to help you effectively integrate a skill into your practice. This is not a mentor's job. If what needs to be accomplished is quantifiable via a checklist, you are very likely talking about coaching.

Coaching is essential to helping us get better. There have been several great things said and written about coaching. Books, blogs, articles, doctoral work, and so much more has been shared about the value of coaching in education.

First-year teachers need to branch out beyond their coach and immediate surroundings to create mentoring relationships, as do all teachers. The two separate and distinct relationships will serve different roles in your development throughout your career. Without cultivating both, you create a hole in your development, which can lead to lack of growth and burnout.

This chart shows the two distinct relationships.

	Mentoring	Coaching
Definition	A complex, voluntary relationship built on mutual trust and respect, developed over time covering a variety of areas	A relationship based upon developing one or more specific skills in an individual or group
Goal	To produce a difference in experience	To produce a difference in skill
Expectation	Both parties are expected to grow and develop through the relationship	Coach affects growth in individual or group

What is Mentoring?

A mentor relationship requires an understanding of the whole person; cultivating those relationships should begin as we are being introduced to the field of education. Despite our exposure to many different teachers during the pre-service period of teacher education, many of us come into the field without having a single true mentor in place.

While some of us may accidentally develop these relationships, the path to building valuable mentor/protégé relationships is largely neglected. Our Teacher's Journey is incredibly difficult. How have we neglected to teach our newest educators, or any educators for that matter, strategies to determine who will best mesh with them as a mentor?

Engaging in effective mentor relationships is challenging even for those of us who know what we need. Novice and pre-service teachers are typically still learning about their own style, as well as the various crafts employed in good teaching. If we are going to develop as educators, we need to know both what and who we can find to foster that growth. This process should have begun before any of us left college.

One of the most vital tasks of teacher educators is to help them plant their seeds. Education is constantly evolving. Some argue that the pendulum merely shifts, but in truth, the field is constantly in flux. What we need as novice teachers when we leave college will not be what we need in year three, year five, or year ten. Instead, we all need to develop a garden of potential options for growth. By developing relationships with many educators, we will set a foundation that leads to both quality mentoring and quality coaching experiences.

Creating these connections is not only a function of exposure, but also of experience. In other words, provide opportunities for both coaching and mentoring relationships to grow throughout our Teacher's Journey. We, as teachers, are best served by both meeting and engaging with many educators, and by learning in an atmosphere where mentor/protégé experiences begin taking place at the beginning of our Teacher's Journey, and continue throughout our careers.

In most pre-service programs, potential educators are required to observe several different teachers before a student teaching experience. Doing this exposes us as future teachers to a small variety of educators. Of the perhaps five teachers we they spend time with, will we truly be compatible with each? Of course not. It is possible we might not be compatible with any of these potential mentors. Essentially, this system creates conditions in which we have a very small pool of people to draw upon for help, guidance, development, and growth. Looking at this pool of potential coaches and mentors leaves us with very limited options, as we begin the most challenging stages of our journey.

Even with this pool, we, as new teachers, seem to neglect the good people we have encountered upon our journey. How can we be expected to continuously develop mentors who help us grow if we are never taught to identify them? There is no need for you to be alone as you tackle the challenges of your Teacher's Journey, no need for isolation. Finding mentors needs to be an intentional part of our journey, not just haphazardly stumbled into.

In some programs, students are encouraged to reach out to the larger education community. Doing this well expands the pool of our potential mentors exponentially. By creating connections outside of the placement schools, you increase the chance of finding educators who fit your style and personality. You also increase the likelihood that those educators have something of value to add to your practice, not just in the novice stages, but throughout your career. How might we encourage this practice from the beginning stages and throughout our careers?

As teaching changes, so will your personal professional development needs. Changing needs and increased learning can often cause the mentor relationship to alter the nature of the relationship altogether. Having multiple options to develop mentors and seek out coaches is not only logical, but necessary. As new teachers develop into journeyman teachers, master teachers, and ultimately into retirement, their needs change, as will their needs for mentorship and guidance.

In addition to exposing teachers to many quality educators at the beginning and throughout their careers to expand potential mentor pools, we must also give

them experiences with quality mentor relationships.
This can be extremely difficult because the relationship
must be voluntary, and the two sides have to gain
something from it. Creating these circumstances
artificially in the pre-service term may require some
forced structure in the beginning. Once the structure is
successfully in place, however, the culture of
mentor/protégé relationships could take root and
create many genuine experiences for future educators.

You may wonder what this looks like in the
earliest stages of a Teacher's Journey. Creating that
experience could take many forms. One possible
iteration could look something like this:

Future teachers entering the program spend
planned time together with those who have recently
completed their first year. Likewise, aspiring educators
heading into their practicum observations would spend
time with those who are preparing for student teaching.
The progression continues until those in student
teaching are frequently meeting with educators from as
many areas as possible.

While this may not create truly authentic
conditions for mentoring at the outset, over time, the
culture of the program would become one where
program veterans give back to those who are coming
after them. Either way, it creates the potential to grow
and experience those relationships in a more structured
environment. Once the teachers leave that environment,
they are going to need to able to successfully identify
mentors and find ways to build those relationships.
Practicing these skills during their undergraduate or

pre-teaching experiences would be incredibly valuable.

Mentors, Coaches, and The Teacher's Journey

How does all this relate to my journey as an educator? The role of mentors and helpers along the Hero's Journey is well-outlined. Luke had Obi Wan; Frodo and Bilbo both had Gandalf. The reality is very few great things are accomplished individually. Within your Teacher's Journey you will undoubtedly face many obstacles, struggles, and micro-journeys throughout your career. You need not, and should not, encounter these trials alone. It is important to identify the who, what, when, and where of your journey to navigate it successfully.

Coaches make our success possible. While we can learn things on our own, coaches know the ins and outs of skills we are just acquiring. I could learn how to navigate the school information system all on my own, or I could just have someone show me exactly how to do it. I could learn to use gamification in my classroom, perform a valuable observation, or complete required state compliance forms all by myself. But, why? The time it takes learning these skills independently and without the assistance of a coach could be better spent elsewhere.

I am not saying let someone else do it, nor am I advocating you sit and get your learning. Simply be aware that when you know someone with a specific skill set, leverage that skill set. Are you working with a new software or trying to get quality 3D prints? Use a coach.

A coach's role is to impart skills from their
knowledge base to yours. You can pay them, they can
volunteer, or some variant in between. Your
relationship with the coach doesn't need to be a
personal one, it merely needs to allow for the transfer of
new skills which you can then implement. Professor
Snape is an excellent example of Hero's Journey coach,
not for Harry Potter, but for his classmate Hermione
(Rowling, 1999). She loathes Snape, yet he has
tremendous skill at potion-making, and she learns many
of those skills from him while in his classes.

How can we identify coaches? This is easier than
identifying mentors. Pay attention to what skills you
want, and who does them well. Ask specific questions
like, "When I am making 3D prints, how do I clear a jam
in the nozzle?" Does this person have that skill? Will
they help you learn it? If so, you found a coach!

Also, look for specific feedback from
administrators and assigned coaches. If I am there to
help you learn to use Google Forms, guess what? I am a
coach. Come back to me and ask for my help when you
are using Forms in your classroom. This is a vital role in
our improvement as educators. Listen to feedback,
identify where you need to improve, and seek insight
from those who do it well.

Like mentoring, coaching isn't something that
should take place only when you are new, and then
never again. It should be taking place continuously as
you grow in the profession. Do not assume that because
a coach has finished sharing what they know that you

cannot return to him/her for help. That return is what starts to build the relationship that lays the groundwork for mentoring.

Identifying your mentors can be a bit harder. Again, you were probably assigned a "mentor" from the first day of your career. That person was likely a teacher in your grade or subject level. They were typically a veteran or master teacher, and as we have discussed, might have had a checklist of things to make sure to show you. Wait, they have a checklist of "stuff you need to learn" filled with specific things like how to take attendance? Sorry, that person is a coach and not a mentor, not yet anyway.

There is no rule that says a coach cannot become a mentor, but mentoring isn't done with a checklist, and it isn't assigned to you. These are points I cannot stress enough. **Only you can choose your mentors.** Mentors can only make themselves available for the mentee, but forcing the relationship can lead to strain and struggle.

The mentor relationship is unique. It isn't based upon lists, skills, or requirements. As Army Veteran Dr. Ray Kimbell describes, mentoring comes from a relationship developed due to a difference in experiences, is built upon mutual trust and respect, and is chosen by the mentee (Kimbell, 2015).

It isn't about where you fall on the scale, how long you have been working, or even what title you hold. Mentoring is about experiences, trust, and respect. Identifying mentors is about collecting good people. At any given time, I am building relationships with other educators. I often draw from their personal experiences

to improve my own learning and development. Building
the relationship and developing trust is where you start
the mentoring process. Identify good people around
you, especially those who seem open to being helpful.
Start engaging with them. Get to know what they offer
regarding experiences, not just in the classroom, but
also as a person. Mentors are people you are going to
trust with your deepest concerns, struggles, and
hardships. They will also share in your greatest
personal successes. Successful mentor relationships
don't end when the difference in experience ends. They
continue as friendships.

The First Time a Mentor Saved My Career

In my first year of teaching, I was assigned a
mentor. I liked her personally, but as I have mentioned,
we didn't mesh professionally. I was a little different
from the start, and from a 20-year veteran who had
been doing much the same thing for the past ten years, I
just didn't see how it was going to work. She shared a
lot of her resources with me, and we would talk about
our families.

From the beginning, even though I didn't realize
it, we were building a relationship. While I didn't love
many of the resources and would alter them or make
my own, I kept coming back to talk to her. I didn't really
have "a person" at the school. I was new. People were
nice to me, but rarely did anyone come in and offer help,
so I went to her.

After nearly half a year of getting to know one

another and having her share resources with me, I found myself in a very difficult situation. I was starting to get frustrated with my "mentor" because she wasn't giving me any of the skills I felt I really needed. She had books, curriculum materials, and other things that I didn't. Her style, her lessons, and her materials that she did share often did not fit with mine. But I still liked her personally. We had talked at length about her family, my family, and life in general. I had stopped asking her most "school" questions. I didn't love how her answers worked for me, so I found ways to do it on my own. It was one day, however, in one moment, when her mentorship saved my career.

I had a class that provided numerous challenges my first year, not just because it was my first year, but because of the various needs and personalities that mixed in the classroom. On one occasion, I sent a girl to the office (forgive my new teacher struggles), mainly because she was crying inconsolably over a small event that happened in class. She was asked not to do something and was presented with an alternative. She didn't accept it and then cried hysterically. It happened more often than I'd like to admit in that group.

I sent her to the office to essentially remove her from the environment and allow her to reset, which typically worked well for her. She was sent back shortly after that, when she proceeded to do exactly what she was asked to stop in the beginning, prompting another similar episode. Deja vu...

My administrator told the girl that doing the original activity would be fine, despite my saying otherwise. We had a short, but cordial disagreement when discussing it, and I moved on. Less than two hours later I received my state evaluation paperwork from my administrator. She had crushed me on that evaluation (one that would earn me full certification) and specifically mentioned my inability to communicate. I was dumbfounded and disillusioned. I could not believe someone responsible for my growth and development would use an evaluation as retribution for a disagreement. (Again, excuse my first-year naiveté.)

I talked to my wife and my parents (both former educators), and yet I still wasn't sure what to do. I was right about this incident. I was RIGHT! How could I let this horrific injustice slide?

My parents suggested that I talk to my mentor. I scoffed a little. We got along, but we were very different teachers. How could she possibly understand this? My parents asked, "do you trust her?"

So, the next day I spoke with her. I told her everything. I asked her what I should do. This wasn't a skill I could learn; this was her expertise and experience in knowing how the political landscape of the school worked. She told me she would support me either way. She told me that my administrator liked me and was invested in my success. This would blow over, IF...

...if I swallowed my pride and inflated sense of injustice.

I went into the administrator's room, smiled, said, "Ok, I will work on it and do better," and signed the paperwork. I took her advice. It wasn't easy. Remember, I was a gift to education, and here I was signing an evaluation as if it were a court ordered admission of guilt. But I did it.

Four months later, the school was desperately trying to save teachers' jobs. The State of New Jersey had cut about one billion dollars from the state education budget, and to keep teachers, the school would need to hike real estate taxes in the small town by nearly 35 cents per $1,000 of valuation. The budget was defeated. Meeting after meeting, day after day, I waited to find out if I would have a job in the upcoming year. I was preparing my applications to other districts.

During this time, I tried to focus on doing my best in the classroom while I was there and preparing to apply to new jobs when I wasn't. Some of those jobs were outside education, which was incredibly frustrating to me. It had taken me so long to find my first job, and so many experienced teachers would be looking, that it seemed I might bomb out of education in year one.

Each meeting, my administrator stood in front of town council members and angry people who talked about how they used to go to school with 80 kids in a class. People literally counted the cars in the school parking lot one day as a justification for cutting staff. My administrator stood toe-to-toe with those people, and defended my job with a passion that convinced the people who mattered most in the room. My administrator saved my job and in doing so, saved my career in education. I am forever grateful for that, along with many other things she did for me.

Would she have done that if I had protested this

"clearly unfair" evaluation? If I had filed a grievance and fought her on it? Most likely not. The advice of my mentor changed the course of my career. I trusted her, I respected her understanding of how the school worked, and I drew upon her experiences to make the right choice. Doing so saved my career. I admit to never having thanked her for that. It is my guess that she doesn't know the profound impact it has had on my life and my career.

Several years later, my mentor made some remarkable changes in her teaching practice. She did so with the help of a younger teacher who was able to mentor and coach her in those dramatic shifts, and she was named Teacher of the Year in our district. Being a mentor doesn't depend on your age or years of service, but on your experiences that you can share with others.

Mentoring has an incredibly powerful impact on our profession, if done well. It should be the norm in our culture rather than the exception. As a profession, starting at the school and district levels, we need to develop a culture of mentoring throughout our careers to create better teaching and learning on a larger scale.

The Next Step

Changing the way we look at mentoring and coaching is a big shift in our mindset in education. Building up each other and focusing on how we can help one another needs to become the norm. When we start seeing mentoring and coaching as resources we develop ourselves, we will stop leaving so many educators in isolation.

We will start breaking things down in a slightly different way for the next few chapters. As we pause to reflect and take actions to help us improve, we will focus from a point of growth.

Mentees (Not Manatees)

All of us need someone. Learning how to find that someone and make good choices about how they can help you is important to long term growth. Here are some things that can help anyone at any stage:

1. Acknowledge that you can't always succeed as an educator by yourself. You can always benefit from a mentor at ANY point in your life.
2. Consider changes you might be expecting in your life, your classroom, or your school over the next two years.
3. Identify people you know who have been through similar changes.
4. Reach out to one or more of those people, maybe not to talk about your anticipated changes directly, but simply to remind them that you are around. Rekindle any relationships you may have with those people and continue to do that periodically.

Mentors

While I often make a point to explicitly say that

anyone can benefit from having a mentor, it is equally
important to point out, especially to our newer teachers,
that ANYONE can BE a mentor. Anyone with a greater
level of experience with something than yourself can
potentially be a mentor. Start learning to mentor others
early on!

1. Think about what you have experienced
   in the last few years. Did you have a
   career change, major shift in the way you
   run a classroom, major life events? Any of
   those experiences can provide an
   opportunity for mentoring.
2. Be available. If you spend some of your
   time focusing on building relationships
   with your peers, staff members, and
   members of the larger educational
   community, mentoring opportunities will
   grow organically.
3. Know your limits. You can't, nor should
   you be, a mentor for everyone. But, you
   can keep the relationship open for future
   scenarios. Also, since you are collecting
   your good people, be able to help refer
   someone to a potential mentor.

Coaches

This whole concept can be a hard pill to swallow
for coaches. As coaches, we are told that our
relationships matter with other people. I don't want to
claim that they don't. But, I can learn from a coach

without liking them. I can acquire skills from a coach without having high levels of trust and respect. Coaches are however in a unique position of having countless opportunities to develop mentoring relationships by the design of their roles. Here are some important strategies:

1. Don't force things. You will need to share your skills with other teachers, but forcing a deeper relationship will often keep it from building on its own.

2. Expect that some people will be very open to you and hope to draw on your experiences. Others won't be ready. They may need mentors who are closer to their own potential changes with whom to develop a relationship. Try to point them in the right direction.

Return: Giving Back to
the Ordinary World

Chapter 8

A Culture of Mentoring

Imagine a school where teachers at every level understand how to seek and develop mentor relationships; a place where no teacher is left to navigate the perils of the journey alone. What does this magical place look like in practice? How do we really build this culture? It starts from the first days of a teacher education program.

I have heard people talk about how important relationships are for student learning, but so often we neglect to pay attention to the relationships when we address adult learning. We ought to start teaching the next generation of educators how to develop relationships, not just with their students, but also with their peers, and with the good people in their lives.

I have met several young teachers from various teaching programs in education. Each time, I try to impart to them the importance of collecting good people. I encourage them to identify the people you meet in their placements who are willing to help, to develop relationships while you are still in the program, and find ways to stay in touch with those people after graduation.

As I have mentioned, some of the most well-prepared teachers I have encountered have come from Rider University and Dr. Michael Curran's classes. What they all seem to have in common is a thorough and diverse set of teaching placement experiences and connections to the education world.

Dr. Curran's classes investigate topics in education and share their learning on Twitter. He amplifies his students' voices and provides them with an opportunity to interact with professionals in the connected world of education. We live in a world that allows us to connect with anyone, anywhere, anytime, and yet we still allow new educators to survive their tests and trials in isolation.

Dr. Curran's students have a tremendous advantage when leaving school because he gives them a voice and a pathway to find good people. If more new teachers entered the profession with a network of potential mentors, they would find the journey less about survival and more about self-discovery and growth.

As the journey progresses, we ought to exist in both worlds at once: we can simultaneously be mentors and mentees. As a continuous learner, I am always hoping to improve on some aspect of my practice, to make shifts in both my classroom and my life.

Personal and Professional Networks

During your journey, it is important to realize you are not alone. Part of cultivating your awareness of potential mentors and coaches is to engage in and develop personal and professional networks. Over the past several years, I have developed many of these kinds of relationships. While some of them are separate, they tend to overlap where I find a few people in many of the same groups. There is a danger there in hearing the same voices. It is interesting to learn from so many different people and to hear so many great voices in contributing to a digital space.

We need our people. In the past, those people had to be in close enough physical proximity to you to develop a relationship. Those relationships were what helped us survive the difficult times and inspired us to be successful during our careers. Unfortunately, you may not always be able to find your people in your own physical space. With the world of opportunities that are available to us all in our current environment, sometimes we need to find other people outside of our immediate space.

No matter what your path, style, or personality, there is no longer a need for you to go it alone. I have already talked about my early years and the difficulty of being alone. I wasn't completely alone in education. I had a few people with whom I could seek counsel and share frustrations and successes. But as I grew and developed as an educator, I needed different things. In the first group were still people I appreciated were still friends, but their role in helping me grow professionally had come to an end. That is the beauty of great mentoring relationships; they can easily remain great relationships long after the mentoring role has passed its usefulness.

This did however, leave me with a hole. I needed new mentors. I needed to find people who could help take me through different phases of my teaching journey. Each new step was one that someone else had likely experienced, but very few of those experiences were shared with people in my local school.

Where to turn? How do we find these mythical mentors who can alter our paths? I found the people I needed in a few different spaces, and I found them through a combination of luck and naivete. My MSA (Master of School Administration) professor Dr. Spike Cook would talk about using Twitter for professional learning.

Outrageous! Everyone knows Twitter is for stalking celebrities and giving athletes the means to destroy their careers in 140 characters (now 280). Surely there was nothing to be gained in this space for a teacher! But, I gave it a shot because I liked Dr. Cook and I needed to learn more about the man whose given name was Spike.

I jumped into this new, odd place without a second thought. In short order I found the accounts of people whose books, blogs, and other contributions I had read. Remarkably, I received personal responses from all of them. They would read my writing, answer my questions, and even share my ideas. While few of these individuals became true mentors, the idea that so many people were ready, willing, and able to engage with my thoughts and ideas was inspiring.

Within a few months I had really started to

collect many of the good people out there who fit what I needed. Some of them even collected me! Others just happened to be in the same space at the same time. We would talk, share ideas, and ask questions of one another. Over time, we developed relationships that went beyond acquaintances who mere learned in the same space. Through amazing events like EdCamps, the annual ISTE conference, and other educational gatherings, we had to chance to deepen our connections by meeting in person. Over the years, the various groups and relationships I have cultivated have overlapped, increased, and developed into a vital part of how I grow and thrive in my Teacher's Journey.

Twitter was simply one of many avenues for finding people. I have found people via a variety of social media tools and at events and conferences, and I continue to seek out local connections. Over the years, I have developed hundreds of relationships with people who might become potential mentors, coaches, and regardless, friendships. These are people who at times I can help, or at times help me. Knowing who is out there in the world to call upon when some new challenge arises can make a huge difference in your ability to tackle that challenge.

I am not alone in this endeavor. Neither are you. Like me, you will be able to find many people who can help you and who you can help. This is the culture we need in our field if we are to be successful in our individual Teacher's Journeys. It is a culture that others have learned to embrace, share, and promote.

Cori Orlando, a TOSA, or Teacher on Special Assignment, in Simi Valley, California has been embracing that culture through writing, presenting, and social media. Cori's story isn't unique, but it is important. She, like myself, found it amazing to see how the people who have been pushing the needle in education over the past several years were so personally accessible. Not only were they not different than anyone else, most of them treat everyone as someone from whom they can learn. While there are the occasional few who have forgotten what life was like before they met the right people along their journey, the vast majority of people in this space are open and willing to share.

Cori uses a commonly heard phrase to describe her experiences: "Finding [her] Tribe." When she talks about finding people, she doesn't mean that she was actively looking. Finding one's tribe is an organic process. Her tribe is a randomly assembled group of great people who she has come to know through cultivating relationships. As she reached out to them, they made themselves available to her. Now she has relationships with several incredible educators all over the world.

One of the most important lessons Cori shares is to reach out to others. She has reached out to leaders in our field. What did she find when she reached out to top authors, award-winning administrators, and organizational leaders? She found friendships, mentors, and more.

"At a time when I needed it, I got a call from one of my mentors. They were honest, but that honesty came from a place of caring. It was what I needed to hear." These are powerful words. What makes them so important, what makes mentor relationships work, is that advice and honesty come from a place of caring and respect. Without as base of trust and respect as a prerequisite, the best advice in the world could easily go unheeded.

Understanding Life Balance

"I need to find a good work/life balance" is something you have probably heard someone say, if you haven't said it yourself. Truthfully, I have said that myself many times. Then I realized the hard but liberating truth: **Work/life balance is a myth** created from a misguided understanding of what balance means. It implies that there is some separation between your life and your work.

When you think of balance, if you are like most people, you imagine some perfect 50/50 split of yin and yang. This imaginary harmony is detrimental to your success and your health in your teaching journey. While you may at some points in your journey achieve the perfect balance, that is a mere snapshot of a person in motion. Think of balance instead like a tightrope walker. Balance is the act of constantly readjusting yourself along the path. While you may feel yourself leaning too far in one direction or the other at times, the key is a simple readjustment. When people tell me that they are struggling to find balance, I ask them if they've fallen.

It is hard for people to think of work in this way because they want to think of their job as something wholly separate from their person. The reality is that any activity you spend doing for a third of each day or more is bound to become a part of your identity.

As Kory Graham has said many times to me, "any activity that you are passionate about is bound to unbalance your life at some point." If you are hoping to be "balanced" and you are invested in your journey, you will always find yourself frustrated with the result.

I have repeatedly seen chats online, been a part of many conversations, and constantly pushed the envelope in the discussions about the work/life balance issue. I do so because we do ourselves a disservice when we attempt to think of balance as two sides of a scale that line up perfectly. We are not loading two things separately and trying to see how they fit.

Instead, the tightrope walker is the better analogy because we are trying to keep balance, moving ahead while outside forces cause us to move to one side or another. Work is not something separate from your life; it is a part of it. While at times work can seem to consume you, you are so much more than your work. At the same time, trying to separate it, as if being an educator were not an integral part of who you are and how you live your life, is futile.

There have been many times in my career that I

seem to have been overly shifted toward school or home. I have left conferences early or skipped them all together. I have been away from my family as I traveled across country, and to other countries, to pursue professional opportunities. Each time, I know that my path has moved in many directions.

Maintaining balance isn't about equality, but about being present where you are needed, when you are needed there. You will have times when your work consumes you and times when your family life prevails over nearly everything else. You need time for you, time for family, and time for work. Neglecting any part of your life in totality doesn't allow you to be successful on the journey. Embrace the constant flux you will experience.

Being aware of what is happening in your life is a huge part of being successful in your journey. Big things happening at home? You are going to have to find ways to pull back at work. Busy time at work? You may find yourself staying late a few extra evenings, or bringing extra work home. That is the simplistic version; the more complicated version comes when you factor in the many things you do within your life altogether.

Thinking this way allows me to identify when and where I will push and pull. It also allows me to look for good times to plan. I keep personal, professional, and educational goals on a chart. I also keep a list of the people involved who can help me succeed in those goals. Again, even in achieving balance, being alone is not the best path to success. Balance isn't about the snapshot in time, but the ability to navigate your

Teacher's Journey successfully. It is about not falling off the tightrope, adjusting when necessary, and moving onward.

Developing Mentor Relationships Throughout Your Life

Again, perhaps the most prevailing misconception about mentoring is that only a novice will need mentors. There is no viewpoint more detrimental to our ongoing success than the idea that we don't need anyone's guidance or support once we have a few years of experience on our resume. Mentor relationships are vital to developing successful teaching, but also to being a successful human being. There should never be an end to our quest to collect and cultivate the relationships we can find with good people. Learning to collect good people should be part of our learning how to be an adult. Whether we learn this in high school, college, or in the professional world, we should know the people around us who can help.

Toward the beginning of our journey, I suggested that no teacher ought to feel alone in their classroom. What can with that feeling of isolation lies in how we find ways to break away from the islands that have confined us to solitude. That process must include mentors. Mentors are the people whom you trust and respect. People who you will keep with you in those times when your ability to navigate the upcoming waters is most in doubt. Rather than maintain the illusion that you will be fine on your own, reach out to those around you who can help.

Complete this exercise in your mind as you read. You are about to make an important decision regarding a major change in your career. Whatever the next potential change is for you, it is here.

1. Who do you know who has recently gone through something like this?
2. Is this a person for whom you have respect?
3. Is this a person you trust?

If the answers are yes, then the person you are considering is indeed a potential mentor. You need only plant the seed by continuing to make contact with that person before you share your concerns about the next step in your career or life. If you have answered no, there is no point in going further; look for someone else. If you are not sure, that becomes a challenge. You will have to invest in this person to some degree. Spend enough time talking with him/her to determine how you feel about him/her as a person.

Why don't we consider the mentor selection process more often? Making authentic connections takes time and can be difficult. It is, however, extremely important to being successful in the journeys of both our careers and our lives.

How do I do it then? It goes back in some ways to understanding what you want in life. Think about it, plan for it, but also be open. When I think about the professional hopes and personal dreams I have, and what it will take to make those things a reality, I am in a significantly better starting place to identify potential mentors (and yes, this ought to be plural). As you go through life and meet people about whom you can answer "yes" to questions two and three, keep them around. Maintaining those relationships requires meaningful conversations at times, but often simply saying hello to remind them you still value the connection between you is enough to keep that relationship going.

It may be difficult for you to plan who and what you will need going forward - or maybe it isn't difficult at all. What matters is that as you meet and begin spending time with new people in your adult life, you make decisions about them as someone you trust and respect, or someone you don't. Keep the first group and reach out to them occasionally. This is how you develop mentor networks. This is how you will avoid feeling alone when going through the greatest trials of your journey.

Creating the Next Generation of Mentors

At this point, we have established how vital the process of mentoring is to all our growth and development. But from the youngest educators, to the veteran teachers who are ready to pass the torch, mentoring needs to be a vital part of the story. Despite how important mentoring is for successful growth, so many people are unprepared not only to find mentors, but also to become a mentor for others. For our profession to grow to its potential, we need to grow master teachers who can foster the growth of the future educators.

You may think I am being overly dramatic. For the most part, this is about your own journey, about figuring out your own needs and how you can grow. But as I mentioned earlier, I truly believe that part of our responsibility as professionals is to find ways to give back to our profession. If you love education chances are you already are the type of person who contributes to the field.

If more of us were willing, capable mentors, the profession would be in better hands. So, the question remains: how do we do we build the next generation of mentors? It starts with us. It starts with building our own ability to mentor. How do we make ourselves available for the next generation and foster their growth?

I can think of several ways I have changed my approach to mentoring. When I first wanted to work with other teachers I would go to their room, let them know who and where I was, and offer them any help I could give. I would make a point to stop by and check in on them. I realized that this was exactly what everyone did for me - and the very thing that frustrated me as a new teacher.

When I first started my career as a teacher, people were nice; they came by and asked if I needed help and told me to check in if I needed them. I was offered a vague promise of help, but I wasn't even sure what I might need help with, so I had no idea what to ask. What nobody really did well that first year was to listen to me. They all offered help, they were all nice, but nobody showed they could listen. Nobody really showed me a reason I should trust them.

My second year, this improved, thanks to what started as a collaborative relationship with our Speech Language Pathologist, Amy Sack. Amy started out simply talking with me about lesson ideas. We built trust and became friends. Amy had experience that I couldn't match, and she had proven to be trustworthy. She built trust by sharing with me first about her family, her frustrations, and her hopes. After a whole year, I finally had someone who I could talk to at work about difficult situations that came up. She didn't always have the answers, but she did listen. I trusted her, respected her, and worked with her to try and make things better in our school for several years.

The mentoring relationship I developed with Amy was both a professional one and a friendship. I realized later that building mentoring relationships wasn't just about telling someone you would help them; it was about listening to them, even when you weren't helping you with a specific professional problem. It was about trusting them so that they could trust you.

I have always had the desire to work with and help others coming into teaching. That desire is built from the strong interest that people took in helping me early on in my career. As I have grown throughout my career, I appreciate the help I have gotten from others along the way.

Looking back, it doesn't seem like a normal thing for a principal to take so much stock in the development of an aide who wanted to be a teacher. Nor was it necessary for so many of the teachers I worked with to invest in my development, but they did. Because of that, I have wanted to help other new teachers develop and succeed. Early in my career, I was terrible at it. Part of that was my need to learn more about being a teacher, but part of it was my inability to understand how to mentor.

Mentoring is as much about listening and availability as anything else. From my own mentoring experiences and my repeated attempts to make myself available to other beginning educators, I realized that mentoring is more than teaching someone. Developing relationships as a mentor can be frustrating. You don't get to choose the mentee. They choose you. And because they choose you, all you can do is listen and be available. As the relationship develops, you may find mentees coming to you. You may not even realize you are in a mentor role for them. I don't tell my mentors they are mentors; I simply continue to work on building a relationship of trust and respect. When the relationships are in place, solving the difficult problems becomes much easier. If we all make ourselves available and become better listeners, the mentoring relationships will take flight, and this will become the norm within our generation and the next.

Making ourselves better educators is important, not just for our kids or our schools, but

for ourselves. It isn't just about being better ourselves, however, it is about giving back to the education community. Modeling mentoring, teaching new educators how to find mentors, and helping them learn to become the next generation of mentors will create a culture that improves education on a large scale. Remember though: it starts with you!

The Next Step

Creating a culture of mentoring and professional growth will aid us on our journeys. At each step along the path we have both something to offer and something to receive. While we explored those concepts in previous chapters, here it will be important for us to reflect upon and understand life balance. Life balance is a skill we all need to continuously develop, yet one we often misunderstand and struggle to find.

1. Let's start with your calendar. How do you plan things? What goes on your calendar first? I am about to make the same radical suggestion to you that I make to kids: Start by scheduling what you love most. You are going to do those things anyway, you might as well not try to overbook them with work. Every weekday from 4pm till around 8pm is typically family time. While I may still have a hard time avoiding obsessively checking my devices, that time is RARELY used for work. My kids are awake, and I

want to invest that time with them as often as possible. Any personal work, or even school work that I may need to take home, typically gets scheduled around that. Start your schedule with things you love most, and you will end up in fewer times when you frantically need to get something done at the last minute.

2. Look at your life on a longer timeline. Think about what you want personally, professionally, and educationally on a timeline for several years into the future. Of course, your plan may change, but having a plan gives you the opportunity to see where one area of your life may start to invade more heavily on the others. It gives you the chance to prepare for your future and think about who will be able to support you in it.

3. This is a theme from earlier in the book, but learn to say "NO". "No" doesn't have to mean "never", and it doesn't mean nobody can do it. Failing to say no can mean you don't give an aspect of your life the full attention and dedication it deserves. Being able to say no allows you to focus on the things that matter to you most in each arena of your life.

4. Collect good people. I know what goals I have, and because I have thought them out, I also know any number of people

who can help me achieve them. This becomes even more important when you start to find ways to keep balance throughout your life.

Chapter 9

Multiple Heroes' Journeys

Now that you have seen the Teacher's Journey unfold, and how in each stage we progress through challenges that alter us along the path, you will hopefully see the parallels in smaller versions of the Hero's Journey. Your micro-journeys can take place in many ways and concurrently throughout your career. Seeing smaller versions of the Teacher's Journey will allow you to find your way through many challenges. If you are still not sure how this applies to the rest of your world, don't worry; the micro-journeys will become apparent.

Your Year as a Mini-Teacher's Journey

Up to this point, we have talked about the Hero's Journey, and the subsequent Teacher's Journey, as it extends throughout your career. We have walked the path from receiving the Call to Edventure through developing into a master teacher and back home again. All the while, we have experienced the challenges, the struggles, and the triumphs of the Teacher's Journey.

Despite all the exploration of the journey, we have not yet spent time identifying its arc in other aspects of our professional lives. Yet, if we recognize the key aspects of our own journeys as they show up on a small scale, the challenges we overcome in smaller increments will be achieved at a greater level.

As you depart, your call to adventure is the promise of a new year. Whether you are excited about the year or have concerns, the year is coming. You are being propelled towards your next journey.

During the school year, you start with the known. You plan your classroom and create a general plan for how you think your year will go. There may be kids' names on a list, curriculum changes to address, and all the details that you go over to start the year.

As you begin, you plunge into the unknown. As you forge new connections with students, learn of the challenges you will likely face, and start to find your paths in the journey ahead, the cycle really begins to take shape. As the year builds up and you figure out what you are having trouble with, it is a perfect time to call upon your mentors or create new mentor relationships. These relationships will help you pass through the newest things you learn and use during the year.

In every year, there is at least one moment that challenges you beyond the normal difficulties. I have come through on the other side of many of those severe challenges, the "abyss" of the hero's journey, where we are not sure how everything will turn out. I have shared some of those moments, and in truth, so many of the most powerful moments came in my last two years of teaching. The abyss was so deep, the connections were so close, that the experience each time changed me.

I have shared stories about some of these challenges, losing my classroom and the hours I had spent remodeling it, the tragic death of a former student whose brother was in my class, and many other challenges. From working with students who live in unsafe homes, to children whose families are displaced from their homes due to drugs and addiction or natural disasters, each year can bring harrowing challenges. **Our job is so often beyond what is in the description.**

A few years ago, I had a student whom I had worked with for two years. That child lost his father figure (his grandfather) to suicide in the late spring. This kid was always a little difficult to work with; he was incredibly intelligent, but never made things easy. He reminded me of myself in a lot of ways. Sitting with him just to help him cope with life was one of the most difficult things I ever did as a teacher. I had no idea what to say to him, and no way to make it better. I couldn't tell him it was going to be ok. All I could do was sit with him, tell him he was loved, and let him be him. I told him I would do that anytime he needed for the rest of the year.

I don't think of that time as a win, as having succeeded in teaching. If anything, I felt like I lost. I lost whatever innocence was left in that class. My students had dealt with the death of a child, abuse, drugs, and more. They had been hit by cars, suffered emotional trauma, and who knows what else. I always thought I could help, that I could come out on top, but I couldn't. Sometimes you complete the journey with death and rebirth. I lost. That young child with so much potential was beyond my reach. All I could do was sit with him while he survived something I couldn't take away from him. We made it through the rest of the year. He did the best he could, and so did I.

That summer I had an opportunity to move into a new role with a different district, and I had to take advantage of that for my family and myself. I still often think about the student I mentioned above. I wonder how he is, if there is anything more I could have done. The amazing thing about the year as a Hero's Journey is that you don't always "win" the major conflict; sometimes you don't come out on top. But you are reborn, arriving back at the next new year a little stronger, a little wiser, and a lot more capable of beginning the next journey.

Each year is different and comes with an incredible collection of hopes and challenges to address. Understanding the cycle of the Hero's Journey can help us understand the ups and downs we face throughout the course of our school year. It can also help us to figure out how to achieve the goals we have set, navigate the most difficult stretches, and help those in our care to succeed.

Each of us in on our own unique journey throughout the year and the years ahead.

But, as you think about the flow of a year, you will start to recognize the landmarks, the places were typical challenges arise, the periods where you can count on smooth sailing through calm seas for long stretches, and when your greatest challenges will pop up. If you've taught a few years, you have undoubtedly experienced the strong periods from January to March when there are fewer disruptions; the natural challenges of the year seem less overwhelming. You have also fought the monsters of Spring as the weather may warm and students can see the home stretch at the end of the journey. How do we use that knowledge to help our kids and ourselves?

Knowing yourself is important for so many reasons, but understanding your strengths and weaknesses needs to go beyond only skills. When was the last time you seriously thought about how you function during different the parts of the year? There will always be unexpected giants to slay, but we shouldn't allow regular occurrences to become impassable mountains in our year.

While so much of this book is focused on people and on knowing who we are, it is also about being intentional with our actions. Part of being intentional is understanding what you need, what you don't, and how you create changes to build greater experiences for yourself and everyone with whom you work.

Our Kids as Heroes

It is easy to get lost in your own journey. Sometimes things are so challenging, we have a hard time seeing all the other concurrent journeys that are happening as we walk our path. Not only are you on your own Hero's Journey, but everyone around you is on their own journey as well. Some of those journeys mirror yours. Sometimes you can work with others to build a stronger team for the challenges that will undoubtedly come. It can be easy to forget that this doesn't just apply to teachers. Each school year is an archetypal hero's journey for your kids as well.

Our kids come to school each fall. Often, they have no choice in the matter; they are literally thrust into the journey without their choice. They are paired up with potential helpers and detractors, and asked to accomplish great feats.

One of the most rewarding aspects of our work is the ability to be the mentor for so many young people on their own journeys. Part of our job is to help them overcome the obstacles they face. There will always be a debate about the lengths to which it is appropriate for a teacher to go in helping their kids. Are we overstepping our boundaries?

But those boundaries aren't stone; they are more like sand. The winds of context often shift the line. I see my role as more than just the person who gives kids tools and skills to learn, but also shepherd them through challenges and prepare them to be as successful as possible life.

Throughout the course of the journey for our young, unsuspecting heroes, we can help them learn through our experiences. Our ability to share our personal experiences with kids is often crucial to their success and our ability to work with them. Talk to your kids, learn about them, and share your experiences. You have valuable life experiences that kids don't have.

That being said, be mindful of who your students

are and what their experiences have been. You aren't there to save them or to fight all the battles for them. You are there to guide them, to provide them with the ability to be successful later in life. You are not the hero; you are the helper. The sooner you embrace that role for kids, the more likely you are to find success.

Kids will always have varying perceptions about school. Some leave the experience inspired; others frustrated. How we work with them can help change some of those perceptions. Most of this book is about you. It is about how you can understand yourself and your role in the world of education. But understanding the Hero's Journey concept can also help us understand where we are needed. In all this talk about teacher preparedness, learning, wellness, and growth, never forget:

You are not the hero in anyone else's journey.

You are almost always one of three things: a mentor/helper, a detractor, or the ultimate struggle of the abyss. Which one you are to a child can make all the difference in how their journey continues, so think carefully and choose wisely.

Micro Journeys Throughout Your Year

Just as our whole lives, careers, and even individual years can be seen in the frame of the Hero's Journey, so can any new learning we hope to do. We can use the cyclical nature of the journey to understand the difficulties that may be ahead, and we can learn to find people who will be able to aid us in finding success. New learning, especially new learning that we hope to implement in our classrooms or schools, can be filled with unexpected challenges and roadblocks.

Seeing the learning experience as a departure from something you normally do helps us keep perspective on the cycle of how we learn new things. Our micro Teacher's Journey is a series of learning challenges that often need support to achieve success. The eventual end where you either master the learning or find that it isn't going to work in your classroom is the return in your micro Teacher's Journey.

Sometimes we choose to take on the new learning; other times it is required of us. Either way, we are starting on this mini journey with the expectation that what we are learning will benefit ourselves, our students, or both. For that to be the case, we need to be able to implement that learning effectively. Anyone who has tried to implement something in their class knows it is not a single occurrence, but a process. Being successful is more than just getting a new concept or material in the hands of your kids. That is, of course, an important start, but just getting something out there isn't enough for it to be successful. Success means using the learning and mastering it in a way that you can adjust it to the needs of your students and yourself.

Part of success in new learning is growing in ability to make changes to the shifts that a classroom requires. If you truly understand something, you can find ways to adapt the concepts you have learned to whatever you need. Finding mentors and coaches can be invaluable in this process. Mentors help you with the experiences they've had when implementing new learning. They can share their failures, how they have been able to adapt the concepts to fit their needs, and how to avoid pitfalls before they happen. The coach can give you the skills to use the learning. The combination of the two can help you take that new learning to new heights.

Finally, if you have become effective in this new learning, you can give back. This step is often missing from new learning, and it is one that districts are so desperately hoping to find. How often are you sent to a workshop and asked to "turnkey" some new skill? Of course, that is ridiculous. You went to a workshop given by someone who (theoretically) has put this new learning into practice in a classroom, and soon after you are asked to reproduce this learning for others. You haven't had the chance to really learn the material, or to apply it effectively in your classroom. That is where so many "turnkey" attempts fail.

When you have returned wiser, more experienced in the new learning from a full journey cycle, you will be able to teach people more effectively. This is where we can give more back to our fellow educators. You become the mentors, the guides, for new learners that can implement this new learning in their classrooms.

The Hero's Journey cycle can be seen all around us. It can be used to understand and be intentional about our careers, our years, how we help our kids, and any new learning we undertake. This isn't the only way to see the world, just a way to structure what you see to allow you to be deliberate about how we can do more than simply survive.

The Next Step

This chapter in and of itself is a major point of reflection. We can see the journey all around us. It can take place on smaller scales, and it is taking place for other people each year. Recognizing how to help others along their path is an important. We can either help them or hinder them; the choice is ours.

1. When you are beginning a new year, or a new experience, look to recognize the journey components. Start learning to use each stage as an opportunity.
2. See where others are along their own path each year. Recognize that while you may not be the mentor, you do have a role to play. Will that role be a positive one?

Chapter 10

Call to Action

So here we are, having walked through the cycle of the Teacher's Journey many times. Throughout this book, you have seen the Teacher's Journey reflected in my stories, as well as those of other educators. We have walked together along the journey, pointing out key aspects and moments along the way. The path hasn't always been clean, and it varies for each of us. What is important is that we identify in ourselves and others where we are and how to be successful along the journey.

If you haven't realized yet, I have been your mentor on this mini Teacher's Journey. You have been reading, finding pieces with which you identify, taking that which you need and leaving the rest for another day.

While many of the stories in this book focus on my journey and my experiences, **I am not the hero in this story. You are.** Yes, you, the one reading this book now. How can that be?

Simply put, we are all the heroes of our own journey. It may sound selfish in some ways, but it is quite the opposite. You must remember that while you are the hero in your own Teacher's Journey, you are merely a character in the journeys of others. Which part will you play? Will you become an aide to these would-be heroes? Or will you become part of the obstacle that becomes their great ordeal? Either way, you are part of the story. Which part you play in others' journeys remains to be seen.

Within your own journey you have many choices, but being the hero isn't one of them. You are the center point of your story. You are the one upon whom the trials will fall. How you navigate those challenges is a major plot twist in your own mythical story. Use the experiences in this book, learn from the examples of others, and find a better way forward for yourself. At the very least, learn how to avoid being alone in education. While we all might benefit from independence, we do not ultimately benefit from isolation. Identify good people in your life, collect them, and learn to accept their guidance and support when you need it.

As the hero of your own journey, here is my challenge to you. Get to know yourself. Start to learn what you love, what you need, and who can help you get there. You can take control of your journey. Understand your challenges and what changes you are likely to face. Avoid the pitfalls where you can by learning from others. It can be easy to become overloaded by the myriad of things you will be bombarded with along the way. Learn to say no, but learn how to say yes more effectively as well. Each day focus on the things that matter in your life, both personal and professional. Use that focus to accomplish the small steps of the journey that lead to great distances over time. This is how you will stay balanced on your path, how you will find what works for you.

As a character in the journeys of others, choose to be the light. Choose to find ways to help others along the path. Make yourself available, as a good person, to share your experience and expertise with others. Many teachers often feel as though they have nothing to share, but this could not be further from the truth. As we all experience our own journey, we gain incredible experiences. Someone somewhere is also struggling to find the way through an experience you have already mastered. Allow them to learn from you. Allow them to keep you in their corner. This is one of the most crucial ways that our profession will grow and continue to develop in the future.

My second call to action for you is one of giving back. Where can you help others to be successful in their own journeys? Can you work to create an atmosphere in your classroom or school that focuses on supporting others in their journeys? Remember try not to be all the things, but to focus on those things you truly love and then build from there. Who can you find? Who can you build a connection with that will help them?

As the world races forward, our human connections to experiences and each other will help us improve. Those shared experiences are what will bind us together rather than tear us apart. Go forward. Find new paths along your Teaching Journey, and remember to light the way for others. You are both the hero and the spiritual aid. Find where your contributions fit in the education world, share them, and build the profession to greater heights.

References

Bolman, L. G., & Deal, T. E. (2010). *Reframing the path to school leadership: A guide for teachers and principals.* Thousand Oaks, CA: Corwin.

Bouffard, S. (2017). Riding the turnover wave, *Usable knowledge: Connecting research to practice,* Retrieved from: https://www.gse.harvard.edu/news/uk/17/08/riding-turnover-wave

Campbell, J. (1993). *The hero with a thousand faces.* London: Fontana Press.

Dudley, D. (2010). Every day leadership [Video file]. Retrieved from https://www.ted.com/talks/drew_dudley_everyday_leadership

Kimbell, R. (2015). It takes more than rank to make a mentor, Army Magazine, Retrieved from: https://www.ausa.org/articles/it-takes-more-rank-make-mentor

McGuire, K. (2015). As veteran teachers face more time demands, placing student teachers grows more difficult. *Star Tribune,* Retrieved from http://www.startribune.com/as-veteran-teachers-face-more-time-demands-placing-student-teachers-grows-more-difficult/293771361/ .

Rowling, J. K. (1999). Harry Potter and the sorcerer's stone.

USA: Scholastic Books.

Simon, P. (1973). Kodachrome. On *There Goes Rhymin' Simon* [7' Vinyl]. Columbia.

Winkler, M. (2012). What makes a hero [video file]. Retrieved from https://www.ted.com/talks/matthew_winkler_what_makes_a_hero

About the Author

Brian Costello, owner of BTC2Learn LLC, is a Google Certified Innovator & Trainer in his 11th year of teaching in Southern New Jersey. His career started as an instructional aide before going on to teach Kindergarten, 1st, and 2nd Grades. He now works as a middle school Digital Innovation Specialist in Egg Harbor Township, NJ.

Brian is the author of the highly acclaimed book, *The Teacher's Journey,* and hosts a podcast by the same name. His innovation project, The Global Audience Project helps classes find, and be, authentic audiences for projects around the world.

Brian is an avid writer, blogger, and social media user. He has also published two children's chapter books: Will McGill and the Magic Hat and Will McGill and the Costume Calamity. He has also published for the NJEA Review, CUE Blog, and as a contributor to the *EduMatch Maker Book* and *Fueled by Coffee and Love*. Brian has had the opportunity to share his learning in the United States and Canada on topics including educational technology, leadership, communication, and professional development.

Other EduMatch Books

Why do you? Why would you? Why should you? Through the pages in this book, Dene Gainey helps you gain the confidence to be you, and understand the very power in what being you can produce. From philosophy to personal experiences, from existential considerations to the very nature of the human experience, consider who might be waiting on you to be you.

We're back! EduMatch proudly presents Snapshot in Education (2017). In this two-volume collection, 32 educators and one student share their tips for the classroom and professional practice. Topics include culture, standards, PBL, instructional models, perseverance, equity, PLN, and more.

Made in the USA
San Bernardino, CA
07 July 2018